Ben's Book
of Miracles

by

Ben Lippert

ASPECT Books
www.ASPECTBooks.com

World rights reserved. This book or any portion thereof may not be copied or reproduced in any form or manner whatever, except as provided by law, without the written permission of the publisher, except by a reviewer who may quote brief passages in a review.

This book is sold with the understanding that the publisher is not engaged in giving spiritual, legal, medical, or other professional advice. If authoritative advice is needed, the reader should seek the counsel of a competent professional.

Copyright © 2012 Ben Lippert and ASPECT Books
ISBN-13: 978-1-57258-804-2 (Paperback)
ISBN-13: 978-1-57258-805-9 (ePub)
ISBN-13: 978-1-57258-806-6 (Kindle)
Library of Congress Control Number: 2012933465

Published by

ASPECT Books

www.ASPECTBooks.com

Contents

Chapter 1: The Early Years 7

Chapter 2: School Days 13

Chapter 3: Conflict at Home and Abroad 20

Chapter 4: A Miracle and Mr. Anderson 30

Chapter 5: Youth 36

Chapter 6: Bittersweet College Days 44

Chapter 7: Heartbreak 50

Chapter 8: New Beginnings 61

Chapter 9: Hardship and Angel Choirs 70

Chapter 10: Working for God, Rototilling to Pay the Bills 79

Chapter 11: Lay Evangelism Work 88

Chapter 12: My Weakness, God's Strength 95

Chapter 13: Faith that Moves Mountains 102

Chapter 14: More Faith that Moves Mountains 107

Chapter 15: Ripples on the Water 111

Introduction: Why I Chose to Tell My Story

Solomon said, "Truly the light is sweet, and it is pleasant for the eyes to behold the sun; but if a man lives many years and rejoices in them all, yet let him remember the days of darkness, for they will be many. All that is coming is vanity." (Ecclesiastes 11:7, 8)

Everyone's journey, in this life, encompasses both good and bad. My life has been filled with both joy and sorrow. Many times my faith has been shaken, tested, and tried. Since accepting Christ as my personal Saviour, I've felt overwhelming despair and even been tempted to turn my back on God.

My God is a miracle-working God. He answers my prayers and He wants to answer your prayers, too. What is the secret to having God answer your prayers? There is no secret. Jesus often told those whom He healed, "Thy faith hath made thee whole." (Matthew 9:22) We must have faith. If you know you are destitute even of faith, why not pray the prayer of the desperate father recorded in Mark 9:24: "And straightway the father of the child cried out, and said with tears, Lord, I believe; help thou mine unbelief."

This book is my response to the unbelief I see in people around me. There is a God. He is my dearest Companion. The miracles He has done in my life are proof that God exists and loves me so much that He sent His Son to die for me. Not only that, but He is interested in my personal struggles and often intervenes to help me. Atheism and the theory of evolution are knocked flat in light of these things.

In these few short pages I have recorded just some of the miracles God has done in my life, but I must say with John:

And many other signs truly did Jesus in the presence of His disciples, which are not written in this book: But these are written, that ye might believe that Jesus is the Christ, the Son of God; and that believing ye might have life through His name. John 20: 30, 31

So, reader, if you don't know God, have never heard of Him, or have turned your back on Him, I earnestly pray and sincerely desire that as you read through the following pages, you will come to an understanding that God does truly love and care for you, too. If your faith in God is firm and strong, I pray that as you read through the following pages, your faith will be strengthened all the more for any tough times that may lie ahead.

Ben Lippert

Chapter 1: The Early Years

Birthplace and First Memories

I was born August 9, 1927 in Bassano, Alberta. In our family, there were four girls and I was one of two boys. My first three siblings, Henry, Elsie, and Clara, were born in Hilda, Alberta. After that my parents, brother, and sisters moved to Bassano, which is famous for the Bassano dam, and there the next three children were born. Lily was the fourth child, after her I was born, and Ruth was the sixth child. I was born and grew up during the depression years on the southern Alberta prairie.

During this time we grew a very large garden. We watered the garden from our own well which we pumped by hand. Pumping water was very tiring work. It was necessary to do this daily because the ground was sandy. When the harvest began and the watermelon, cantaloupe, and muskmelons were ripe, we would haul them into Bassano and would sell them from house to house with a horse-drawn wagon or sometimes a Model-T, which I learned to drive at the age of eight. When the rest of the garden produce—potatoes, turnips, peas, beans, etc.—was ready, we also gathered it and carted it off to town to sell.

The Little Preacher

And these words, which I command thee this day, shall be in thine heart: And thou shalt teach them diligently unto thy children, and shalt talk of them when thou sittest in thine house, and when thou walkest by the way, and when thou liest down, and when thou risest up. Deuteronomy 6: 6, 7

From the time I was two-and-a-half years old until I reached the age of five-and-a-half, I was called "The Little Preacher." My parents used to stand me up on a chair. I had only heard three sermons which were about Daniel and the lion's den, Belshazzar and the handwriting on the wall, and the three men in the fiery furnace. I would stand on the chair for several minutes and sing and preach to anyone willing to listen. I no longer recall my words.

We used to go to the blacksmith, Mr. Sheltsky, and he would say to me, "You can't preach." "Yes I can!" was my emphatic response. We'd go back and forth like that for a bit and then I would preach to him and sing songs for him. After that he'd always give me a coin for my preaching and singing. As a child I thought about God often and really enjoyed looking at the night stars while I thought about Him. From the earliest I can remember I was deeply impressed that God loved me.

The First Miracle I Remember Seeing With My Own Eyes

And the prayer of faith shall save the sick, and the Lord shall raise him up. James 5:15

My brother, Henry, was ten years older than me. From the time that he was six years old, he had been experiencing epilepsy attacks. As he got older, they worsened. It got so bad that by the time I was three years of age, if he was having an attack, my parents would have to use a spoon to keep his tongue from going down his throat and choking him. His attacks were a horrible thing to watch. Eventually it got so bad that when they sensed an attack coming on, my parents rushed him in to Dr. Scott in the hospital in Bassano. The last attack he had caused his heart to stop beating and the doctor pronounced him dead. My parents cried.

My mother rested her hands on Henry and began to pray. She prayed that God would heal him and make him well. Henry opened his eyes and said, "Why didn't you let me sleep? It felt so good to be that way." That was the first miracle I witnessed.

The Bassano Church

My parents were both Christians, but there was no church in Bassano. The members in Bassano decided to build a church of their own. They bought an old house in town and tore out all the walls. Money was short and calcimine[1] made the walls nice and bright white. Someone donated an old pedal organ with a leaf on each side. We set an Aladdin lamp on either side of the organ on the leaves and one gas lantern hung from the ceiling. We were able to conduct our services by the light of these three lights.

However, the depression was so strong, that most of the members moved to British Columbia where the weather was better and fruit could be grown. After that we only had a few services in the church. I remember my dad was the last one who spoke there. There had been no crops that year, so Dad decided to leave as well.

We moved to Thorsby. We only stayed there one year. It was so muddy that we lost our horse and cow due to hoof rot. Our animals had not been used to such wet conditions and it took its toll on them. My father got frustrated and moved us back to Bassano.

My dad bought a Model-T in Edmonton. We loaded the running board with a dozen chickens in a box and the dog. My dad had made a four-wheeled trailer out of a car and we hauled that behind the Model-T. What was left after selling what we could was packed into the trailer. It took us three days to drive from Thorsby to Bassano. Today, I can drive the distance in less than five hours. At that time though, the roads were not as good as they are today, the cars were slower and we were hauling a trailer that slowed our progress even more. Every time we came to a hill, we had to unhook the trailer and hook it to the car's front bumper. We climbed each hill in reverse. Then at the top of every hill, we would have to unhook again and hook the trailer back up to the rear of the car before continuing on with our trip.

---

1 calcium and lime powder in water

I remember stopping in Calgary for the first time on our way to Bassano and going into a toy store. Dad bought each of us a present. I got a Mickey Mouse wristwatch. It didn't run but you could spin the hands around and I was so proud of that little watch.

We moved back to the same old house in the country beside the cemetery. It was an old square house with a well right next to it. There was a big pile of dirt beside it from the digging of the well. A windmill was over the hole. My brothers and sisters and I used to play on the dirt pile.

Trapped Headfirst

Children, obey your parents in the Lord: for this is right. Ephesians 6:1

My mother had a rain barrel on the ground beside the porch. It was three feet tall so the top of the barrel was just about level with the porch. In the fall, the top of the water in the barrel would freeze. I wanted to get some of the ice but my mom severely scolded me and told me not to go near the barrel. "You'll fall in headfirst," she told me.

One day while she was doing laundry and the washing machine was making noise, I snuck outside to get some ice from the barrel. I reached down into the barrel and fell headfirst into it. The water was only eight to ten inches deep in the bottom of the barrel and I was able to hold myself high enough with my hands to keep my head out of the water. However, I was unable to get myself out of the barrel. I screamed and hollered for my mother for quite some time until she finally heard me and came outside and saw my feet sticking up out of the barrel. She pulled me out by my legs and promptly gave me the licking of my life. I can still feel it today.

Bicycles and Bruises

For He shall give His angels charge over thee, to keep thee in all thy ways. Psalm 91: 11

My brother Henry used to like catching squirrels, weasels, rabbits, and coyotes and he would skin the hides to sell them. A couple miles north of Bassano there was what people called the "open range." It brings to mind a line, "Where the deer and the antelope play," from the old song, "Home on the Range." When Henry went to catch animals, he used to go to the "open range."

One time I went with Henry. Henry pedaled the bicycle and I rode sideways on the straight bar between the handlebars and the seat. After riding a while, we got to the first big hill which was very long and steep. We had to push the bicycle all the way up the hill. When we got to the top we rode on farther to the range.

On the way back Henry told me to watch my feet as I might get them caught in the spokes because I was sitting on the crossbar. On the way down the big hill, the bike began to move faster than Henry expected. We hit a bump and my foot lodged in the spokes which stopped the front wheel cold and the rear wheel of the bicycle went flying over the front end of the bicycle. I'm sure the Lord's angels had a hand in directing the path of our flight because we landed on the ground right beside a great big rock. I can easily imagine that one or both of us might have died had we hit that rock. Miraculously, neither Henry nor I had broken a single bone. We were very bruised and hurt, yet we both managed to walk home.

Mom, Dad, Me, and the Model-T

During the depression, my dad received $4.00 per month working for a government relief agency. At that time the Honourable William Aberhart (1878-1943) was the premier of Alberta. My dad's job was to work with a team of horses and a Fresno scraper[2] making the Aberhart road which went from Bassano to at least as far north as Camrose. The scraper was used to move the dirt and grass. When the crew reached a spot where a culvert was needed, Dad's job was to make the wooden culverts.

Because Dad was away at work, I had to learn how to drive the car, even though I was the youngest. My mother and siblings would push the car down the slope of the dirt pile and Dad would jump on the running board and tell me what to do and show me how to run the car.

In order to make some extra money, Mom did laundry for others. She would work all hours of the night. She did it all by hand with a wringer washer. We would then take it in to town and deliver it. I knew how to start the car and drive it from place to place and it got so that Dad even told me that I knew how to tune it better than he did. I'm sure he was only flattering me, since I was only eight or nine at the time.

Depression Years

My uncle and aunt came from Thorsby to visit on the weekend that the local rodeo was held. One of my cousins was a bronc rider. This particular weekend he was bucked once and fell off. The wind was knocked out of him and he wasn't moving. I couldn't see very clearly but I thought for sure he had been trampled. Shortly after that he came to and got up. Someone helped him out of the ring and I was surprised when, a little while later, he got on a steer. This time he was bucked twice before flying through the air. He got hurt but he was tough.

We went home that night and the next morning I got out of bed. I had gotten dressed and walked towards the stairs. I stumbled at the top of the stairs but recovered. I walked down the stairs and towards the milk separator where my mom and dad and aunt and uncle were all standing. They had already milked the cows and were separating the milk. As I neared them, I stumbled again and nearly fell into the separator. My mom said, "What's wrong with you?" My father also recognized that something was wrong with me. My feet went in opposite directions and I crumpled to the ground.

After that, a fear developed inside of me. I stopped wanting to sing and was often

---

2   The Fresno scraper was the forerunner of the modern earthmoving scraper. A team of two or four horses pulled it while an operator controlled it with a handle.

fearful that I would experience another "attack" which at that time was thought to be epilepsy (on account of the fact that my older brother was epileptic). When I went to school I stayed near the teacher out of fear that I might collapse again and the other students would make fun of me. Perhaps this was one of the reasons I was so often called the teacher's pet.

Stolen Goods

Ye shall not steal, neither deal falsely, neither lie one to another. Leviticus 19:11

One day my cousin Benny and I were on our way home from school when we went into a store. There were several dollar pocket watches hanging on the board. The owner had gone into the back of the store to look for something and Benny asked me if anyone was out on the sidewalk. I looked and told him no. I didn't realize what he was planning to do. I was shocked when he grabbed four of the watches, stuck them in his pocket, and slowly walked out of the store. Scared stiff, I followed him out. We walked around the building and down the back alley. I kept saying to Benny, "We're going to go to jail." I was really nervous and scared. He said, "Everything will be okay, don't get so excited."

We were nearing the cemetery outside of town and he pulled out the watches and asked me which one I wanted. One of the watches had a black face with gold letters on it. I told him I wanted that one. He gave it to me, then headed to his home, and I to mine. I didn't know what to do with the watch. I stopped at the cemetery and thought that maybe I should hide it in the buck brush. After thinking about it for a while, I finally decided to bring it home with me.

When I reached home I was relieved to see that the Model-T was gone. That meant that my mother and father weren't home. I went into the kitchen and fiddled with the watch. I wanted to wind it but it was already wound tight. I was so preoccupied with it that Mom and Dad returned before I had time to think about where I was going to hide it. Quickly I ran into my mother's bedroom and shoved it into the pillowcase. I must admit it was a dumb place to put it. We weren't allowed to go into our parents' room.

Afterwards I wanted to get into their room to get the watch and hide it in a better place. I kept trying but my mother kept catching me in her room and scolding me. My parents sent us kids to bed and I worried that they would hear the watch ticking when they got into bed.

There was a vent in my room to let up hot air from the downstairs. From it I could watch my parents in their room. They blew out their lights and got into bed. I could hear them wondering aloud where the ticking sound was coming from. They lit a candle to search for the source of the strange sound. After they discovered the watch, they called my siblings and me downstairs. They asked, "Who took this watch?" None of us answered but mothers have a way of reading their children.

My mother looked at me and I began to cry. Through my sobs I managed to say that Benny had stolen it and had given it to me. I got a terrible licking and was sent to bed.

The following day I had to go to Uncle John with my mother to tell him that Benny had stolen the watches. I was so scared. Uncle John was a mean man. After my mom told Uncle John the story, Benny had to go get the watches. Uncle John jumped on Benny and started beating him. My dad had to pull him off to stop him from hurting Benny worse than he already had.

The next day we had to go back to the store to return the watches and apologize for stealing them. I was frightened. I figured that even if we returned the watches, we would be put in jail. We went into the store and my mother did most of the talking. Benny and I apologized. To my surprise, the owner was very nice and appreciative that we were returning his property.

Chapter 2: School Days

Big Valley

My parents decided to move farther north where the climate was wetter and we would be able to grow crops. So we moved onto a farm about twelve miles east of Big Valley. We couldn't afford to keep our car and I cannot recall whether we sold it or just left it behind.

We sent our cattle and three horses by freight train and we came on a passenger train. Once in Big Valley, we rode the horses and drove the cattle out to the farm.

We farmed three quarter sections that we rented from Mr. Hawkins. It was hilly country. The crops grew nicely and we began to make a little living. We still couldn't afford a car so we had to drive the twelve miles to town with a team of horses. To go and get groceries that far with horses was a long trip.

While we were isolated in the Big Valley place, Pastor John Neufeld visited us occasionally. He had a slide projector that he showed Bible illustrations on, but we didn't have electricity. We had a big hog fence around the house and we had to take the fence down in the corner and let him drive his car up to the window. Then we'd put the projector's cord through the window and hook it up to his car battery. He only had a strip of yellow pictures. One of the pictures was supposed to depict the Garden of Eden. Then we'd sing, "Beautiful Valley of Eden". He'd play the organ, he'd just paddle like mad and we'd sing,

> *"Beautiful valley of Eden,*
> *Home of the pure and blest,*
> *How often amid the wild billows*
> *I dream of thy rest, sweet rest!"*

Those visits from the pastor were our substitute for church. I longed to belong to a church family, but it was another ten years or so before I ever got to go to church regularly.

19 Hill

There was a hill about a half mile from our place. It was called the 19 Hill, because it was on section 19. During the wintertime there could be anywhere up to 75 people at one time on the hill skiing and sledding and having great fun. When springtime came we missed being able to ski and toboggan on the hill.

My brother Henry decided to make a wagon that we could ride downhill during the summertime. He got some press drill wheels and made a tricycle out of solid planks. His contraption was so heavy we couldn't pull it uphill without the help of one of our horses. My cousins had come up from Bassano. Ben, the bronc rider, got talked into going on the first ride down the 19 hill with Henry. They weren't even halfway down the hill before the wagon began to bounce to and fro. The wheels got caught in a badger hole and Ben flew off the wagon. The wagon overturned and I was sure it landed on my brother's chest. Henry wasn't moving. I flew down the hill toward him as fast as my legs could take me, crying all the way. After a little while he came to and began to groan in pain. The wagon lay broken in pieces.

Ben picked himself up and said, "I've ridden a lot of broncs and bulls in my life but none have been so rough a ride as this one has been."

Ozark School

Render therefore to all their dues: tribute to whom tribute is due; custom to whom custom; fear to whom fear; honour to whom honour. Romans 13:7

I went to the Ozark School with my sister, Ruth, and about thirteen other students. It was a really rough school. We had three teachers in one year. The first teacher we had at that school was Mr. Merritt. He would tell us our assignment and one student or another would challenge him saying, "Just try and make me do it." All the students used to stand up in defiance against him. He wasn't there long before he just quit. The next teacher was young Mr. Sorenson. The students treated him just the same way they had treated the first teacher. I remember seeing him standing at the window, crying. Not long afterward, he quit. The next teacher was a lady. Her name was Miss Hotzinger. We used to call her "Hot Singer" because she had a wonderful singing voice.

Playing Hooky

"Be sure your sin will find you out." Numbers 32:23

Once, while Mr. Sorenson was the teacher, we hatched a plan to play hooky. The stampede was on and nearly all of the students wanted to go to the stampede. They told Ruth and me to tell the teacher that they had to stay home to do farm work for their fathers so they wouldn't be in school that day. Our classmates said that if we lied for them, they would lie for us so we could play hooky the next day. We did as they asked but the teacher didn't believe me, my sister, and the other two kids that were with us.

The following day it was our turn to play hooky. It was a hot day and we drove by the school looking the other way. We had to go past the school otherwise my father would know that we weren't at school. We had decided that we would tell the teacher that we were looking for a black cow. We went a mile or two down the road and had to keep the horse in the ditch because there were no trees between us and the school and we were in plain view of the teacher the whole time.

We kept checking to see when school would be over. We were so hot and thirsty we couldn't think straight. The day we played hooky turned out to be the longest day of our lives. We anxiously waited for school to be finished. We saw the students spill out of the school and thought for sure it was the end of the day. We started heading towards the school and just as we came near to it, the bell rang. We quickly turned around and galloped back to where we had been before.

Again we waited for what seemed like a lifetime. By and by all the students came out of the school once more. Not knowing that it was only lunchtime, we headed towards the school and as we passed it, we kept our heads looking in the opposite direction as though we were still looking for the "cow".

We were a half mile north of the school in the direction of home and we thought we could hide in the bushes. We weren't really paying attention closely and my dad happened to come down that way with a team of horses and he saw us. "What are you doing over here?" he asked. Quickly I replied, "We're looking for rocks for science." He said, "You can pick rocks later. Come home with me and pick potatoes. I need your help." We were already hot and thirsty and then we had to go work in the hot sun picking potatoes all afternoon. We wished we'd never played hooky in the first place.

Miss Hotzinger

One Friday, my sister Ruth and I had to stay home to help dig out all the vegetables from the garden and carry them in to the cellar. We went to school the following Monday but no one was there and we couldn't figure out what was the matter. Finally, Mr. Stewart, who was a member of the school board, came by and said that there was not going to be any school that day. Eleven of the students had been expelled the previous Friday for using barbed wire to tie the teacher to the post by the well. Mr. Mahaffy, who lived near the school, had been about a half mile away and had noticed that something seemed out of the ordinary. Debating whether or not to check it out, he decided to come by and take a look. That's when he found Miss. Hotzinger wired to the post. For the next three years, there were just four students at that school—myself, my sister Ruth, Millie Winkler, and Reggie McAdam.

During my time at that school we didn't learn to play outdoor games like football. To this day I still do not know how to play any of those games properly. Instead we used to play a lot of indoor games like "Hide the Thimble." Of course we didn't use just a thimble. Someone would hide the thimble, or some other object, somewhere inside the room and the first person to find it was the next person to hide the thimble. One day someone had hidden it in a high spot. I spied it high up on the window. I crawled up onto a bookshelf, but the bookshelf broke away from the wall. I fell down headfirst and broke my left arm just above the wrist.

I didn't realize I'd broken my arm until I noticed it was just hanging. It was wintertime and cold. The teacher rushed me home to my folks. Dad hitched up the horses and we headed for Big Valley. That winter the roads were in terrible condition. Some snowdrifts were so deep that the horses had to jump through them and the sleigh would jerk. The horses got awfully tired. By the time we made it into Big Valley it was dark.

At that time the only doctor in Big Valley was a vet, so we went to the vet. He looked at my arm. Then he grabbed it and pulled. I screamed and hollered. He took two slats and placed one on the bottom of my arm and one on the top of my arm. He wrapped cloth around the slats and said, "Come back in eight days."

Eight days later we returned. He took the slats off and I thought my arm would fall off. He repositioned the slats and I kept them on my arm for another six or eight weeks. I do wish my arm had been doctored properly though, because I always wanted to play the violin. However, because of the way my arm healed my wrist could not turn the way it needed to in order for me to play. For a while I tried to learn right handed but the music teacher told me it was too hard because I was doing everything backwards. I eventually gave up on that dream.

Gratitude

I am often grateful to Miss Hotzinger. She always had a story or poem about God. Many times she would say, "Benny, this is for you." I remember one poem that went like this: "Poems were made by fools like me, but only God can make a tree." She always seemed to point me toward religious things and help me to think of God. The Lord seemed to do that for me at every school I went to. One of my favourite poems is "Abou Ben Adhem" by James Henry Leigh Hunt. That poem had a lot to do with how I felt about God. When I turned the lights out at night, I thought of the poem and felt that God was near me. He was a comfort to me. I wanted my name in the book of life. The poem really spoke to me.

Back in those days, the whole class would say "The Lord's Prayer." Afterward, the teacher would read an easy to understand portion from the Bible. She was a nice Christian lady and was always trying to help us remember how much God loved us. Her efforts helped me to keep thinking about God. When she quit teaching, we cried. For years afterward, she sent us Christmas cards. Even after I got married, I was still receiving cards from her. Later I lost track of her and I'm sure she is no longer living.

The Teacher's Surprise

O God, thou knowest my foolishness; and my sins are not hid from thee. Psalm 69:5

I was responsible for the janitorial duties at the school and I did my cleaning in the mornings before school started. In the winter, it was also my duty to light the fire in the mornings to warm up the room before the teacher and other students arrived.

To pass the time till school started, the other boys and I discovered that if we put an unspent bullet on the stove top, it would explode once it got hot enough. Either we found the bullets in the woods or we took some from home. Anticipating the bang and discovering the resulting hole in the ceiling was always quite a thrill.

One morning on my way to school, I found a 45[1] calibre bullet. It was big. I could hardly wait to try it out on the stove.

I lit the fire, put the bullet on the stove, and quickly exited to the cloakroom. I waited for quite some time but the bullet did not explode. I spied the teacher heading to the school when she was a half-mile away and I began to get anxious. The teacher drove into the schoolyard and put her horses in the barn and still the bullet had not exploded. All the while my anxiety was mounting. I realized that I had not stacked the fire properly so the stove had not heated up as fast as it should have. I wanted to go into the classroom and remove the bullet, but I was afraid it would blow up when I got there. Soon enough the teacher opened the door and entered the cloakroom where I nervously waited.

I wanted to warn her but I was afraid of getting in trouble. She opened the door to the classroom and just as she entered the room, the bullet exploded.

I ran into the room after her. The bullet had gone through the decorative ceiling plate and right through the roof. I could actually see the sky through the hole. I was so thankful Miss Hotzinger hadn't been hurt. God surely prevented a tragedy from happening that day.

I went back to the school about twenty years later. The school was abandoned. As I came near, pigeons flew, circled around and landed again on the weathered roof. I went into the classroom and pried the ceiling tin plate off the boards and took it home as a reminder of God's mercy and intervention.

Manure, Glorious Manure

There were two barns on our farm that had been built into the hill so that the haylofts were level with the ground behind them. The hill was so steep that, from the front side of the barn, the hayloft was about twenty feet off the ground. At the front end of the hayloft was a little door through which Dad used to toss hay down to the sleigh below. To keep the door closed, it had to be fastened with a little hook latch.

Ruth and I used to have great fun playing hide-and-go-seek in the hayloft. If the hider could sneak to "the hay door" while the seeker was searching, he or she would be considered safe. The seeker would have to keep searching until he or she caught the hider.

One time, when it was my turn to be the seeker, as I counted to fifty, thinking to play a joke on Ruthie, I undid the latch that fastened the door shut. I thought it would be great fun to watch her reaction as the door swung open when she hit it with her hands. While I was "seeking" for her, I purposely went far enough away from the door so she would have plenty of time to "sneak" on me and get to the door before me. When she got out of the hay and started for the door, I pretended not to see her so that she would run really fast to "beat" me. After she had gotten a bit of a head start, I started "the chase." With both hands in front of her, she ran as fast as she could straight for the door. The door swung open when she hit

---

1   This was a very large bullet for a rifle, used for killing deer, pronghorns and other large animals.

it with her hands and before I had realized what had happened, she disappeared from sight.

I ran to the open door and looked down to see her lying on the ground. So sure she'd been killed, I ran to the back doors of the hayloft and ran down the hill all the way around to the front of the barn.

When I got to her, I yelled, "Are you okay? Are you okay?" She was moving and said, "I'm okay. I'm okay."

It just so happened that my dad had piled a bunch of fresh cow manure about two feet thick on the stone boat[2] which was on the ground just below the hayloft door. When she fell out of the hayloft she landed right on the manure pile. It had broken her fall. Never before had I ever thought I could be so happy to see manure. I was so thankful that it had been there to save Ruthie from certain death. I'm sure that God had His hand in placing the stone boat in just the right place so that it would be there when Ruthie fell.

Cured of Epilepsy

One day on my way to clean the school, I needed to go to the bathroom. I wasn't feeling well and I noticed that I passed a worm that was about three inches long. Seeing this scared me and I ran to school as fast as my little legs could carry me. I arrived there so early that no one, not even the teacher was there yet. I felt as though another epileptic attack might be coming on so I ran the whole two miles back home and fell on the bench from exhaustion when I got there.

My parents were able to get the neighbours to take me to the doctor in Stettler with their car. The doctor gave me a week's supply of red worm pills. They looked and tasted like candies. During the first few days of taking the pills, I passed several worms in my stool. Towards the end of the week I was no longer passing worms. After that, I never had another epileptic attack. It wasn't that I had had many attacks (I seem to recall only having four or five), but it was knowing that I wouldn't have any more that gave me great peace. I'm thankful to God that it was something as small as a simple pill that solved that problem in my life.

---

2 Two runners made from 4x4's or 2x6's with boards nailed across to form a flatbed—something similar to a flatbed sleigh.

Abou Ben Adhem[3] by James Henry Leigh Hunt (1784-1859)

Abou Ben Adhem (may his tribe increase!)
Awoke one night from a deep dream of peace,
And saw, within the moonlight in his room,
Making it rich, and like a lily in bloom,
An Angel writing in a book of gold:

Exceeding peace had made Ben Adhem bold,
And to the Presence in the room he said,
"What writest thou?" The Vision raised its head,
And with a look made of all sweet accord
Answered, "The names of those who love the Lord."

"And is mine one?" said Abou. "Nay, not so,"
Replied the Angel. Abou spoke more low,
But cheerily still; and said, "I pray thee, then,
Write me as one who loves his fellow men."

The Angel wrote, and vanished. The next night
It came again with a great wakening light,
And showed the names whom love of God had blessed,
And, lo! Ben Adhem's name led all the rest!

---

3 'Abou' means 'father of' in Arabic, and 'ben Adhem' means 'of the tribe of Adam.' So the name could be an idiosyncrasy, meaning 'A father from the tribe of Adam' which could be about any one of us.

Chapter 3: Conflict at Home and Abroad

World War II Years

During the war, many people were conscripted into active duty. Food and fuel were rationed. Each person or family received a certain number of tickets with which to get either fuel or food.

It became very difficult for people to farm their land properly because every able-bodied man of the appropriate age was required to leave and fight the war. Only one able-bodied person per farm was exempt from conscription in order to keep the grain fields growing.

Because money was always tight, we had to find creative ways to make money. We used to collect all the bones we could find and bring them to the grain elevators. We scoured the fields for cow bones and the bones of wild animals. I don't know what people used them for but Dad and I used to get $7.50 per wagon load of bones.

We also scrounged up any scrap metal we could find. It sold for $20 per tonne. All the metal was sent to refineries to be made into machines and weapons for the war.

The first years of the war seemed pretty bad. We used to listen to a five-band radio. On our radio we could listen to broadcasts coming out of London, England. We heard Winston Churchill thunder his speeches about winning on the land, winning on the sea, and winning in the air. After some time he didn't seem to sound so enthusiastic anymore. The outcome seemed bleak in France and everywhere else.

It was clear that we were in a state of war. Fighter pilots trained in the skies above us. They were usually directly overhead before you knew they were there which was quite frightening. Imposing army tanks were on the highways. We often had to pull over and wait for the tank to go by in order to continue on our way. Jeeps and trucks hauling soldiers from place to place were also a common sight. Soldiers were often marching here and there, practicing and getting ready to go into the war.

Evidence for Creation

And the LORD God said unto the serpent, Because thou hast done this, thou art cursed above all cattle, and above every beast of the field; upon thy belly shalt thou go, and dust shalt thou eat all the days of thy life." Genesis 3:14

We moved again, this time to Fenn. We came there with a couple of hayracks full of all our goods, chickens and other things. Coming from the prairies, snakes were something that really scared us. We only knew about rattlesnakes, we didn't know about garter snakes. There weren't any rattlesnakes at Fenn, but we didn't know that. As we started to carry the furniture into the house, we saw a snake. We all scattered. Dad got a pitchfork, killed the snake and threw it on the fence. We were hardly through with killing that one when another snake came slithering along. Dad quickly grabbed the pitchfork, killed that one and hung it over the fence with the first one.

There was a great big veranda the full width of the house, with wires strung up and creepers crawling on the wires all the way up to the roof of the house. The snakes had made a nest on the ground under the veranda. By the end of the week, we had 42 snakes hanging on the fence.

On Fridays we'd rake the yard to clean it up for Sabbath. We had a big pile of dry stuff and lit the pile and I took the fork and threw the snakes on the fire to burn them up. I noticed on one snake that little bumps started to pop out. I pulled the snake out of the fire to have a closer look. There were pairs of distinct little paws set about four inches apart along the belly of the snake and a couple of bumps on the back of the snake that looked like there might have been wings attached. It kind of validates the Bible, we thought. God had said, "Upon thy belly shalt thou go." The snake must have been able to fly and walk rather than crawl like they do now. People came from all over when they heard about the snake that we had found. People who had said they didn't believe in God said, "This really shows that God is in control." You could see the little paws as plain as could be and top little humps had burst out for the wings. I suppose that if there had been 10 000 snakes, there would have been more like that one. It probably wasn't the only one like that.

The Only German in a French School

There is neither Jew nor Greek, there is neither bond nor free, there is neither male nor female: for ye are all one in Christ Jesus. Galatians 3:28

I began attending a school in which all the students and even the teacher, Miss Moore, were French. The time I spent at that school was awful. Everyone hated the Germans because of the war and I was the only German student at the school. The teacher often instigated the rest of the students in taunting me. Many times she'd put her hand to her forehead and say, "Germans have a low forehead and are not intelligent people." These comments upset me terribly.

One night three students tried to beat me up. I was hooking my horse up to the buggy and saw that they were coming at me. I caught one by surprise. He had his arms out in front of him to protect his face, but I went under his arms and hit him on the chin and he fell down. I jumped at one of the others and scared him. I beat him, and the third one got scared as well. All three of them ran into the school as fast as they could as I chased behind them. I said to the teacher, "There's your Frenchmen for you, three of them scared of one German." I cried all the way home because I did not want to face all the ridicule anymore.

Mrs. Fleshman, an elderly retired teacher, saw that I had been crying and asked me why. I told her about the rough time I was having with the students and that the teacher was insulting me because I was German. I told her about the three boys fighting me. I told her I did not want to go back to school again because I didn't want to endure another day of mistreatment. She told me that the teacher had no right to be causing trouble amongst the students as she was doing and she told me to speak with the teacher and tell her that if she ever treated me like that again that Mrs. Fleshman would report her to the school board and she would be fired.

Coincidentally, the very next morning Germany invaded France. Germany made it one-third of the way into France overnight. The following morning the teacher announced that there would be no current events report that day. Until that day, current events were a daily ritual in the school. I asked if she was cancelling current events because Germany had broken into France. I reminded her that she had made it a point to tell the class that the French were smart and the Germans were not. The fact that Germany had made it a third of the way into France certainly challenged that supposition. After that incident the teacher didn't bother me anymore, and as time progressed, we got along better and better. Things were never great, but they were better.

Approximately forty years later, one of my classmates contracted lung cancer from smoking. Knowing he would soon die, he tried to locate me. When he finally did, he called me and said, "I'd sure like to come and talk with you, Ben. Can I come and see you? I'm down by the Christian school in Lacombe." I offered to meet him there instead, so he wouldn't have to come hunting for me.

When I got there, he told me, "Ben, the reason I came to find you is because of the way we treated you in school. All my life I've been bothered by what we did to you. I have cancer in my throat. I've lived a long time, and I wanted to make things right with you before I die."

I told him that I wasn't holding it against him. We had a good talk and cried on each other's shoulders. I could tell he was dying, not just because he had told me but because I could hear it in his voice. He died shortly after that.

More recently, I returned to that town when I was doing work in the area and went into a restaurant. I saw a couple of older men there. They seemed to be looking at me. Finally, one of them got up and came over to my table. "Are you Ben Lippert?" he asked.

I told him I was. "But I don't know you," I said. "Who are you?"

"Don't you remember me?" he asked. It had been sixty years since I had last seen him. I didn't recognize him, but he recognized me. "I've been looking for you for a long time," he said. "John was looking for you, too, but he couldn't find you either."

"Yes, he did," I said. But I still didn't know who I was talking to. I didn't tell him John had apologized.

"I've been trying to find you, too," he said. "We gave you a bad time at school, and I just wanted to make it right with you."

I pretended that I couldn't remember, but of course I could. I said, "That's fine." We clasped each other, and he told me a bit about his history and how his wife had Alzheimer's, and he was alone. I told him about my wife and her illness. It was really nice to talk with him again.

Guilt is a terrible burden on the hearts of many people. I'm thankful that God impressed upon these two men the importance of seeking forgiveness from those we've wronged. It's important that when we have the opportunity to forgive someone for hurting us that we forgive them freely. It's such a blessing to share in Christ's ministry of reconciliation as 2 Corinthians 5:18 explains, "And all things are of God, who hath reconciled us to himself by Jesus Christ, and hath given to us the ministry of reconciliation."

Cow Moving

It was about the middle of the war, and I was 14 years of age when we moved to a farm just six miles south of Botha. On horseback, we had to drive our cattle from where we were living to our new place. Charlie, one of our horses, was very old. He was a very gentle horse but his get-up-and-go had long since got-up-and-gone. He was such a tired, old horse that even when encouraged to, he would not run.

Our horses needed to be able to work hard doing farm chores, so Dad kept his eye open for another horse to take Charlie's place in the team. We had nearly finished getting the cattle to the farm when we met a farmer who lived near our new place. Dad noticed that he owned a young horse which was full of life and vigour. It was really quite a nice horse and Dad told the farmer that he would like to have it. The farmer thought for a bit and then told Dad that he could have it in exchange for our old horse. He explained that his children were young and just starting school so they needed a well-trained, gentle horse to ride back and forth to school. Since Charlie was both well-trained and gentle, he fit the bill perfectly. Dad agreed and the young horse became ours.

Since I had been riding Charlie, I got on the new horse, named Victor, and we continued driving the cows. After a while, we approached a railway track. It was apparent that Victor was much livelier than any of us had expected. To encourage the cows over the track, I rode Victor back and forth behind the herd until some cows passed over the track. After that, the rest followed. Once they had all passed over, I tried to lead Victor over the track but he refused to cross. I tried to get him to go over from as many directions as I could and he just kept turning around.

All of a sudden he turned and raced toward the track and sailed over it. I hung on for dear life and nearly flew off his back. After that, we got the cattle to the farm without incident.

Caring for McArthur's Farm

My father and I regularly visited Mr. McArthur, the farmer we had traded horses with. Later that spring, he became ill. In fact, he was so sick he couldn't even get out of bed.

His children were small, so there wasn't anyone who could do his chores for him. He had several milking cows so, early each morning, Dad and I would go to his farm, milk his cows, and separate the milk. After that we would hurry home, milk our cows, and separate our milk. Then I would run to school. Mr. McArthur was bedridden for three months. After that, though not fully recovered, he began to come out to the barn and help us. Every day he thanked us for coming. Those sure were busy days. Eventually he was able to handle doing the chores on his own and we didn't go back anymore.

My Little Island Sanctuary

I used to wade across the lake with my dog, Fritze[1] to a small island at the Botha place and sometimes stay there all day. There wasn't a single tree on the place just buck brush and gooseberries. In the springtime there were a precious few wild strawberries. I used to pretend that I was Robinson Crusoe. I had relief from my loneliness and problems at home and at school.

From the time I was a small child, I believed in God and felt a longing deep down inside of myself. I'm sure God puts that longing in each one of us. On one particularly lonely day after my mother had gotten upset with me over something (it seemed to me that she was always getting upset with me) and I was a ways from the house, I recall crying out. I went into the brush and just cried and cried. I went to school crying. I even went under the step at the school and cried there because I was so lonely and upset. That day, I really did feel forsaken.

A Gramophone and Two Starving Boys

When the war started, my uncle joined the army. Before he enlisted, he gave me his Stevenson 22 calibre rifle. Sometime after we had moved to Botha, I visited a farmer about two-and-a-half miles from where we lived. He was kind of a strange man, but he had a gramophone[2] with several records. Ever since I can remember, I've loved music. I told the farmer that I liked his gramophone and records and he told me that he would trade them for my rifle.

I liked his proposition and went home to ask my mother if that would be okay. She took one long look at me and emphatically said, "I will not allow a gramophone in the house. That is the devil's music!" This upset me very badly. I would not disobey my mother but I wanted that gramophone so badly that I went back to the farmer's place more than once after that just to look at it.

One winter day I got to thinking that I would like to go over to the farmer's house and take another look at the gramophone. It was about ten degrees below zero so I dressed warmly. It took me a while to get there but when I did, I went straight to the front door and knocked on it. I waited for a while but there was no answer.

Just as I turned to leave, I thought I heard a child's voice. I turned back to the door and knocked again. This time I could clearly hear children's voices. I tried to open the door but something had been pushed up against the door from the inside and try as I might, I could not push it out of the way.

---

1   Pronounced Fritzy
2   Phonographs utilized a cylindrical record. The gramophone was a phonograph that introduced disk records.

Chapter 3: Conflict at Home and Abroad

I went around to one of the windows to look into the house and spied two little boys sitting half frozen on a bed. A bag of rice was also on the bed and they were trying to eat the rice but they kept spilling it. The scene was so disturbing that I can never forget it.

I crawled through the window and over the bed. The fire in the stove was out and there was nothing in the house I could start a fire with. Thinking that something might be in the woodshed, I went to the front door and found that a sewing machine had been pushed up against the inside of the front door. Because the floor was rutted, the wheels of the machine table had caught and that is why I wasn't able to move it out of the way from the outside. Pushing it out of the way, I went outside to the woodshed, but there was only slack coal, or coal dust, on the ground where the coal had been piled. Finding nothing suitable, I broke some boards off the granary and brought them into the house. I started a fire, put the boys close to it, and got the house warmed up a bit. Then I left and ran all the way home.

I stormed into the house and excitedly told my mom and dad that the two boys were freezing to death over at the farm down the road. "We have to go and save them," I told them. I told my parents that there was no wood or coal in the house.

We drove out to the farm, picked up the children, and drove them to their grandparents' house a few miles away. The boys' grandparents told us that this was not the first time their parents had left them alone. They liked to party and sometimes would leave on a Friday evening and not come back until Monday or Tuesday.

Later on we heard that the government had gotten involved and removed the children from their parents and placed them in foster care.

A Gun for a Gramophone

After we went back home, I told my mother how much I really wanted the gramophone. Again she told me no because it was the devil's music and she would not have it in her home. I told her, "Mom, I did save the boy's lives, please could I have it because of that." When my dad saw that my mother would not relent, he put his foot down and said, "Ben deserves it. He can have the gramophone and keep it upstairs in his room."

After that Mom said, "Well, okay. I don't want you to have it but seeing as you are insisting, I guess I have to let you get it, but you have to keep it in the attic, shut the door, and play it really quietly." I was elated but knew that I still had to wait a few days because the farmer and his wife were still out partying.

A few days later I went to their home and they were there. I traded the gun for the gramophone and the records. The snow was deep and it was cold. The only way to get the gramophone home was to pull it on a sleigh. I placed it and the stack of records on the sleigh and several times, as I pulled my precious load the two-and-a-half miles home, the gramophone fell off. The snow was deep and it was hard work but I was excited and anxious to hear it play. By the time I reached home, it was already dark. Mom reminded me to take it up into the attic and close the door. I worked hard as I lugged the gramophone up into the attic and then I took the records up there too.

In those days, the gramophone needles needed to be changed on a regular basis. I only had a few old ones and I hadn't gotten any others with the gramophone. I tried sharpening the old needles and even tried using stick pins to play the records. As a result the music was scratchy, but I did like the songs. Most of them turned out to be nice hymns and the ones that weren't, I didn't like anyway. After all my mother's insistence that gramophone music was from the devil, it really was ironic that most of the music was hymns.

How My Mother Came to Love My Gramophone

It was cold in the attic, but I wanted to listen to my music so badly that I braved the low temperatures to play it. One especially cold day as I shivered in the attic playing music, I glanced down the staircase only to see my mother listening quietly at the foot of the stairs. Embarrassed that I had spied her, she quickly ducked away.

Apparently she liked what she heard, because a while later she told me that it would be okay if I brought my gramophone down into my room. She said, "That way you can listen to your music without getting cold." She didn't have to tell me twice. Excitedly I brought it down and set it up beside my bed. Before long, I could hear mother singing along with the record as she went about her house work.

One day when I came home from school, I realized that my parents were not home. A short while later they returned with two boxes of gramophone needles which they had purchased for me to use. Mother brought the needles to me and said, "If you want, you could put the gramophone in the living room so you don't have to always go upstairs." I was happy to move it to the living room. After that, she played it more than I ever did. She could often be heard singing along with the songs it played. Sometimes Dad would get so angry and say, "Shut that thing off. I can't even talk to you because you are always singing."

Sometimes Mom would wind the gramophone too tightly and the spring would break. I don't know how he did it, because they weren't easy to fix, but Father would fix it for her every time. The gramophone and the songs were something that the Lord used to touch my heart and soul for eternity and, as young as I was, I knew that He was with me. I had so many songs, but the ones most meaningful to me were, "Jesus Lover of My Soul," "Sitting at the Feet of Jesus," "Building For Eternity," and "In the Shadow of His Wings." I was really blessed by the music. I felt that God was really near me when I listened to those hymns.

The Fight and Prayer with My Father

Wives, submit yourselves unto your own husbands, as it is fit in the Lord. Husbands, love your wives, and be not bitter against them. Colossians 3: 18, 19

By the time I was twelve or thirteen only my younger sister Ruth and I were still at home living with Mom and Dad. All of my other siblings had run away from home because they had tired of Mother and her constant preaching. They had become accustomed to going to dances. Lily and Henry had even become avid drinkers.

One day when I was playing outside, Mother and Father got into a terrible fight. Mother was so loud that I could hear her clearly from outside. She claimed that, because

Dad was too soft on us kids, he was responsible for the reckless behaviour of my brother and sisters and their abandonment of our family. My mother was the kind of person that once she latched onto something, she couldn't let go of it, and she never seemed to stop pestering my father about this one issue. This particular time, Dad put up with my mother's nattering so long and finally became so upset that he stormed out of the house and into the barn. My mother, still angry, chased after him to continue her tirade.

Unable to escape my mother's scathing tongue, my father picked up a neck yoke[3] and began to chase her around with it. She darted to the house crying, "Oh God! Oh God!" with Dad at her heels half the way.

Dad, his face clouded with a look that I sensed was a mixture of disappointment, resignation, and defeat, returned to the barn with the neck yoke held low at his side. At the doors he stopped as though he were unsure of what he should do next.

Observing from just outside the barn, I didn't know whether to go to my mother or father. While I contemplated, I heard my father begin to cry. Cautiously, I approached my dad and by the time I reached him, he was on his knees, sobbing. I put my hand on his shoulder and he said, "Ben, would you pray for me? Mom just won't quit scolding me and I don't know what to do."

I loved my dad very much. I don't remember him ever once speaking unkindly to me. I wanted to please him, yet he had never asked me to pray for him or even with him before. I don't recall the prayer but I do recall hugging my father after I finished. He said, "Thank you," and I told him, "I love you Daddy." I really did love my dad. It always seemed like he was on my side and I was on his side.

He walked me partway to the house but he still didn't want to go in so he returned to the barn which was warmer than outside. Nervously, I went into the house. When I got in, Mom said to me, "Ben, you and Dad get along so well. Please go out and ask him to come inside."

By this time it was dark but I went out to the barn and found Dad. I said I thought Mom was sorry for getting so upset with him because she had sent me to find him and ask him to come back in the house. With our arms around each other, we walked back.

Mother met us at the door and gave Dad a big hug. I was so happy to see them hug each other I started crying. That incident was one of the worst times I can remember in my young life.

A Sawmill and a Crowbar

Finally, brethren, whatsoever things are true, whatsoever things are honest, whatsoever things are just, whatsoever things are pure, whatsoever things are lovely, whatsoever things are of good report; if there be any virtue, and if there be any praise, think on these things. Philippians 4:8

I wanted to make some spending money for summer time, so I got a job working for

---
3   The neck yoke connected to the tongue of a wagon to keep it from running into the horses.

Mr. Anderson. He bought a sawmill at Rocky Mountain House and brought it home in pieces. I'd never before seen how a sawmill worked and certainly didn't know how one should be put together and apparently neither did Mr. Anderson because he said to me, "Ben, I don't know how to put this together. I need you to figure it out for me."

For days I fiddled with the pieces, figuring out which ones went where. Eventually I figured that the carriage had to go back and forth. I was trying to figure out where to put the blade when a visitor stopped by to see Mr. Anderson. It just so happened that he knew something about sawmills. He told me that the blade had to be set in an eighth of an inch and he helped me set it in just the right spot.

After that Mr. Anderson got logs from south of Alix, hauled them home and I sawed them into lumber. We even used some of the lumber I cut to build some cabins. Constructing the sawmill and being the sawyer was a great experience for me.

I even involved some of the church folks in helping me. Harvey[4] was one of those members. At the time he was really having it rough. His girlfriend had broken their relationship and he had turned his back on the church. I could tell that the breakup with his girlfriend was really hitting him hard and I told him that he needed to forget her and get on with his life.

He said, "You have no idea how hard it is to forget her."

"You've just got to," I told him, "or it'll kill you." At the time, I had no idea how appropriate my advice to him was. Ellen White has this counsel for us on page 251, of *Ministry of Healing:* "It is a positive duty to resist melancholy, discontented thoughts and feelings--as much a duty as it is to pray." I wish I could have encouraged Harvey with this counsel from Mrs. White.

One day not long after that, as he worked with me, I could tell that there was something wrong with him. In his eyes blazed a strange fire I had not seen before. "Ben," he said, practically spitting at me as he spoke, "You're looking at me!" I knew something was wrong with him and I couldn't help looking at him.

Grabbing a crowbar, Harvey rushed toward me. Mr. Anderson and I both ran from him around the side of the building. Following closely, Harvey chased us around the building a couple of times. Then he rounded the side of the building again and just walked off aimlessly into the field, seemingly unaware of what he had just done. After that, we went to the house to call the police. The police officers came and took him away to Alberta Hospital, a psychiatric hospital in Ponoka, Alberta.

For several months afterward, he remained a patient there. The medical professionals encouraged Harvey to take up cigarette smoking as a way to relax. By the time he was released, he was addicted to cigarettes. After that, he was never the same and he never returned to church.

---

4   Name has been changed.

Jesus, Lover of My Soul by Charles Wesley (1707-1788)—1740

Jesus, lover of my soul, let me to Thy bosom fly,
While the nearer waters roll, while the tempest still is high.
Hide me, O my Savior, hide, till the storm of life is past;
Safe into the haven guide; O receive my soul at last.

Other refuge have I none, hangs my helpless soul on Thee;
Leave, ah! leave me not alone, still support and comfort me.
All my trust on Thee is stayed, all my help from Thee I bring;
Cover my defenseless head with the shadow of Thy wing.

Wilt Thou not regard my call? Wilt Thou not accept my prayer?
Lo! I sink, I faint, I fall—Lo! on Thee I cast my care;
Reach me out Thy gracious hand! While I of Thy strength receive,
Hoping against hope I stand, dying, and behold, I live.

Thou, O Christ, art all I want, more than all in Thee I find;
Raise the fallen, cheer the faint, heal the sick, and lead the blind.
Just and holy is Thy Name, I am all unrighteousness;
False and full of sin I am; Thou art full of truth and grace.

Plenteous grace with Thee is found, grace to cover all my sin;
Let the healing streams abound; make and keep me pure within.
Thou of life the fountain art, freely let me take of Thee;
Spring Thou up within my heart; rise to all eternity.

Chapter 4: A Miracle and Mr. Anderson

Miraculously Healed

When I was almost fourteen years old, I began to feel unwell. I felt sick constantly and over time, I just felt worse and worse. It was so bad that I was unable to complete my chores. I did not even have the strength to pump water. It was early June, school had not yet let out for the summer, and I was still attending each day. One day I was feeling so horrible that I crawled under the front step of the school building. After the morning bell rang and I still had not come out, the teacher came out and told me that she knew I hadn't been feeling well and that she would get Ruth to take me home to stay for the remainder of the year.

My mother had 21 siblings. Her mother had had sixteen children before passing away and after the death of her mother her father remarried and had six more children with his second wife. Only a few years before I got sick, two of my mother's young half-brothers had died from some unknown illness that produced the same kind of symptoms I was having. It frightened my mother and me to think that I was probably going to die as well.

My parents did their best to nurse me back to health, but they didn't know much about health and didn't really know what to do for me. They took me to the doctor but in those days, there were no blood tests and there wasn't much the doctor could do for me. The only thing he did was take my temperature and give me some pills. In addition to the pills, which I think may have been only Aspirin, the first remedy my parents tried on me was horse milk. Besides the meagre amounts of food I was able to eat (my mother was always trying to force me to eat more), my parents gave me horse milk to drink. It sure tasted awful and didn't do me one bit of good. When they realized the milk was not helping me, they began giving me my mother's homemade chokecherry wine.

I had been running a fever for weeks on end and by fall, I was so weak that I fainted each time I stood up. Realizing they could do nothing more for me, my parents admitted me to the hospital. My temperature only continued to rise. I was told that it even reached 106 degrees. I was so hot and sweating so much that the nurses had to change my bed sheets several times per day on account of them being soaked through.

A Bright Light and the Hand of God

For quite some time I had been praying that God would heal me. After my fever reached a critical point, I began to pray with renewed fervour. I pleaded with God for Him to heal me and I promised Him that if He did, I would tell everyone I met what He had done for me.

Chapter 4: A Miracle and Mr. Anderson

One day, the doctor took my folks aside and told them they should take a picture of me because I probably wouldn't come out of the hospital alive. We went over to McDermott's Studio, a photography studio next door to the hospital. I was having trouble walking, even though it wasn't far. I was so weak I sort of staggered when I tried to walk and even had trouble standing. My folks had to help me. Once there, the photographer took my picture. Then my parents took me back to the hospital.

The evening that my fever reached 106 degrees my parents came to visit me in the hospital. They had come many evenings but that day the doctor had contacted them and advised them that I would likely not live to see another day. My best friend, Mr. Anderson, also came in to visit me that evening. I don't think anyone expected me to live through the night.

The following morning at about 11:00 a.m. as I was praying, I sensed that I was about to die.

Suddenly, I saw a bright light descend through the ceiling straight towards me. The nearer it came to me, the brighter it became. It became so bright, that I prayed God would shield my eyes from it because the intensity was too much for my eyes to handle. Instantly, the silhouette of a hand appeared between me and the light. From the other side of the hand, I could see the light glaring every direction and it stayed like that for a little while and then moved back up again and out through the ceiling.

I lifted up my head, sat up, and said, "I'm healed!" I called the nurse and when she came in she tried to push me back down onto the bed. She figured that I was dying and that adrenaline was coursing through my body causing me to sit up. I told her that I had been praying and now I was healed.

She ran from the room calling for the doctor. When he came in he didn't even use a thermometer. He just touched the back of his hand to my forehead. Incredulously he said, "The fever is gone! He looks apparently healed." Turning to the nurse he said, "This is not natural. This is divine. Give him his clothing and discharge him."

When the nurse gave me my clothes, I praised the Lord. I went home and walked into the house and my parents were both so shocked to see me there alive that they just stared at me. They told me that for the first few moments, they just couldn't believe it was me. They thought for sure that I was a ghost.

I told them I had been instantly healed by a miracle of God. We all thanked God and hugged each other while we cried.

I wanted to go out to see Mr. Anderson. He lived only a half-mile out of town. He was working at the sawmill so I went there to visit with him and when he saw me, he looked at me like he was seeing a ghost. He told me he didn't believe he'd ever see me alive again after the previous evening. I asked him if we could fire up the sawmill so I could send a few logs through just so I'd be able to say I went to work the same day I'd been healed. He said that would be okay. Then we prayed together and gave thanks to God. I sawed a few logs and returned home praising God for His healing hand in my life.

The Bullfrog in the Basement

After my recovery I continued sawing lumber for Mr. Anderson and began building cabins for him as well. Sometimes we would go into the house to take a break or get a bite to eat. From time to time when we were in the house we could hear a bullfrog croaking down in the basement. Mr. Anderson said that over the last several years, the frog would periodically croak. He had tried to find and remove it but he had been unable to locate the creature.

I went into the basement and lay still for a long time. Eventually, the frog croaked and I determined which wall the sound was coming from. Again I lay still as I waited for the frog to croak and when he croaked I was able to more accurately pinpoint where the croaking was coming from.

I called Mr. Anderson who had been waiting to find out what I discovered and I said, "That frog is in the cement wall!" "Impossible," he replied, "It could never survive all those years in there." Then we heard it croak again and the sound was indeed coming from inside the wall.

Mr. Anderson got a hammer and a chisel and we began to chisel a hole into the wall where the sound was coming from. An inch and a half into the cement, we came to the frog in the middle of the cement wall. It seems impossible that the frog was alive, but once we had chiselled out the wall in front of him, he promptly hopped out right onto the basement floor. We caught it and released it outside.

My Second Father

Mr. Anderson's only son had taken up drinking and smoking. This bothered Mr. Anderson badly. It hurt him terribly to see his child rebelling so openly against God. I was at his home one day shortly after he'd learned that his son had made a second woman pregnant. As Mr. Anderson sat in his basement, I began to worry terribly about him. I could see the situation was weighing heavily on him and I thought, from the way Mr. Anderson looked and was carrying on, he just might have a heart attack. He sat bent over on the chair, clenching his fists. His eyes welled with tears.

I counselled him to stop chewing himself up so much over his son's poor decisions. I told him, "You've got to forget it. God gave him a free will and he chooses to do what he wants." I reminded him that God, in His infinite love and mercy, had given His son free will just as He had given everyone else. I said, "We can pray for him, but that is all we can do. We have to leave the rest in God's hands."

He looked at me then and said, "Well, you're as close to me as he is. From now on you're going to be my son." From that time on he called me his son. He was such a great man and I was blessed to have him in my life as my "second" father. I worked with him for about eleven years and was always there to help in the spring with seeding and in the fall with combining.

Chapter 4: A Miracle and Mr. Anderson

Mr. Anderson's Record Maker

Mr. Anderson had a record maker. During his bout with depression over his son, I tinkered with the record maker. While fiddling with it one day, I discovered a record that had been taped to its underside. Mr. Anderson hadn't even been aware of its existence. I removed the tape that was holding it and listened to it. Out came the words of "When the Morning Comes."

The song gave both of us great comfort and over the following years we often sang it together while we worked. Mr. Anderson needed me and I sure needed his influence in my life as well. I felt that something important had taken place but I could not then know just how much I would need him to be there for me in the future.

Movie Shows

Back in my day, theatre movies were called shows. My parents believed it was sinful to go to shows. In Botha a show called "Snow White and the Seven Dwarves" was being played. My sister and I made up a story that we needed to go into town for singing practice then we went to the show. We thought it was a nice film, with no inappropriate content for children.

Years later I went to another show while living in Stettler. This one was called "Rocketship X-M: Expedition Moon" The only reason I went to see it really was because it was produced by Lippert Pictures, Inc. and that intrigued me. There wasn't anything bad about it. In fact, the actors weren't even dressed in space suits and the leading actress sang beautiful songs.

Nowadays nothing is thought of the countless movies being played and how they are affecting the lives of children. Sister White had this warning for families in 1894:

> *In Christian homes a bulwark should be built against temptation. Satan is using every means to make crime and degrading vice popular. We cannot walk the streets of our cities without encountering flaring notices of crime presented in some novel, or to be acted at some theatre. The mind is educated to familiarity with sin. The course pursued by the base and vile is kept before the people in the periodicals of the day, and everything that can arouse passion is brought before them in exciting stories. (Bible Echo October 15, 1894, par. 4)*

If families were in danger then, how much more so are they in danger now? I may not have understood the reasons why my mother disapproved of theatre going, but I distinctly remember how guilty I felt as I walked home from watching it. On my way home I knelt down and prayed that God would forgive me for watching the show.

Touched by God

We left Fenn and moved to a place south of Gadsby. The new place had a barn, a windmill, and a small house. Ruth was still with us then. While we were at this place, she decided to run away from home. I was really upset because all my sisters had run away and my brother had run away, too.

We started going to church once in a while at C. S. McHardy's at Red Willow. When we got to church, they'd ask questions and I didn't know anything about the Bible. At home, the way we studied the Bible was Mom would read it in German and make us read it. We just copied what Mom said. We read from the German Bible, but I didn't know what I was reading. I didn't know the Scriptures. I didn't know John 3:16 or anything. They'd ask questions in the Sabbath School lesson and I'd try to answer something because I didn't want to look dumb. I'd end up with the wrong answer and be embarrassed. If I'd known that Proverbs 17:28 says, "Even a fool, when he holdeth his peace, is counted wise: and he that shutteth his lips is esteemed a man of understanding," I would have kept my mouth shut.

I guess Mother did her best to teach us what she knew, but I had pretty faulty ideas about Christianity as a result. Mother often used God as a weapon against us to force us to do what was right. She often said, "God sees what you're doing." I didn't know God as a personal friend. I was afraid of Him.

It finally got so hot between my mother and I that I ran away. After I was gone a week, Dad found out where I was and he and Mom came over and he told her she was supposed to apologize. I didn't want to go home, but Dad asked me to come home. I had a soft spot for my dad because I knew that he missed me.

My mother gave me a well-I'm-sorry-but-it's-not-my-fault kind of an apology. I went home, but things weren't good. My younger sister ran away, too. She said, "I'm not staying around here anymore." I really missed Ruth when she left and I started blaming my mother. Dad agreed with me, too. He said to her, "It's on account of you that they're all leaving home. You're always rubbing religion in."

Things got worse and worse between my mother and me. One time I was so mad I had a .22 rifle and I chased her around the house. Then it settled down for a while. But within another day or two, she got at me again.

It just happened to be a Friday night. That's always the way it was. By the time sunset came, everybody was mad at everybody. "Do this and polish your shoes!" And, "Do this and get that!" Everything had to be ready before the sun went down. That day, I got into a big argument with her.

My mother said to me, "Your sins are piled up to heaven. Even God doesn't like you." Hearing her say that made me even angrier and I stormed out of the house and walked by the outhouse. There was an ash pile about the size of a small kitchen table and about a foot tall, right beside it and I stepped on top of the pile. The sun had already half set. I was going to curse God and I thought He'd kill me there and that's what I wanted. Then it would be over with. But God had other plans for me.

As I stood there, I felt a sweet presence come over me. It was as though it wrapped right around me and I started weeping. I stayed there until the sun completely set. After

Chapter 4: A Miracle and Mr. Anderson

that I went back into the house and my mother was waiting for me with outstretched arms. She said, "I'm sorry. It's not your fault. I shouldn't have blamed you." I told her that it was okay and that I knew God loved me. "I just felt His presence," I said to her.

Chapter 5: Youth

My Baptism, 1944

My mother was awfully upset that none of her children had gotten baptized. She was always lamenting about this and one time she turned to me and said, "How come you don't get baptized?"

Nearly a month after that awful fight with my mother, I met Pastor Long. He had been told that my family was Adventist and that I might want to get baptized. When I met him, he asked me if I wanted to get baptized. He didn't ask any other questions. I didn't know anything about the Bible. I didn't even know John 3:16. I just thought that if you wanted to be a Christian, you got baptized, and I wanted to please my mother, so I said yes.

A couple Sabbaths later we went out to a creek by McHardy's at Red Willow and several of us got baptized in the creek. The creek was cold and Pastor Long spoke for what seemed a really long time and I sure felt as though I was freezing. I really didn't understand the significance of baptism and what it stood for and what the results of baptism were. Nevertheless I made a promise to God and myself that no matter what, I would stay true to the decision I had made that day. I didn't even have a Bible, and now that I know what it means to be baptized, I have often thought that I should be rebaptized.

Church Pianist

Pastor Long and the Botha church members had brought three or four families[1] into the faith and we began worshiping together at Erskine.[2] My friend, Mr. Anderson, attended the Botha church. Our fledgling church did not have a pianist and so, being musical and knowing how to play the organ, I was asked to be the church pianist. My family did not have a piano at home so being the pianist was a challenging task for me, at least at first.

I discovered that I had to push the keys much harder when playing the piano than I did when playing the organ. Each week I had four songs to learn and play. Despite my practicing, I often did not push the keys hard enough and they wouldn't sound loud enough and sometimes they wouldn't even sound at all. As a result, I would push them a second time. The singing, however, would carry on without me and I'd lose my place. After a number of weeks, however, I got used to the piano and was able to play the songs through without stumbling over the notes. One thing I never could get the hang of, though,

---

1 Two Erickson families, the Maa family, the Ellison family, and others
2 We had purchased the Royal Bank building for our little church.

was playing songs with more than one sharp. These songs I transposed into a key with flats and that seemed to work fairly well.

New Friends

Among the families worshiping in Erskine were other young people my age. I became really good friends with three young boys named Herb, David, and Fergie. We did a lot of things together and, for the first time, I didn't feel lonely and friendless.

The time we spent together was always filled with good, clean fun. We could go out in the evening and never was a dirty joke told. We would sing hymns together. Our favourite hymn was, "Love Divine, Oh, Sing the Wondrous Story." And then something fantastic happened.

She was fourteen and I was seventeen. Her name was Myrna and she was Herb's sister. I fell head-over-heels in love with her. I was at her and Herb's home so much that it became a second home to me. If I wasn't there, she and her brother would phone to invite me to come on out.

Herb and I wanted to become pastors and, along with Myrna, we wanted to get involved with overseas missions. Myrna and I had discussed the topic of marriage and had reached the conclusion that although we weren't yet ready for college, after our college graduation we would get married and then go overseas to Africa as missionaries. Back then, the mission field was most often considered to be Africa.

God's Power is Greater than Nicotine Addiction

But put ye on the Lord Jesus Christ, and make not provision for the flesh, to fulfil the lusts thereof. Romans 13:14

My brother, Henry, and I often worked together ploughing the fields of our six quarter sections. Henry would stop the tractor several times each day for his "cigarette breaks". My brother had been struggling to break free from his destructive lifestyle, but he had been unable to give up cigarettes. Each day that we went to work, I told him to just leave them at the house but he just couldn't bring himself to leave without them. Then one day he said to me, "I won't let you walk this road alone anymore. I'm going to get baptized. I want to be saved."

Not many days after that, we were both working in the field. Henry was driving one tractor with a plough behind and I was driving another after him. Earlier that very day, I had encouraged him to toss his cigarettes in the wood stove and burn them to remove the temptation. So he did. We had ploughed all morning and it was now past lunchtime.

Henry's tractor came to a stop and he hopped out. I couldn't pass by his tractor with mine so I also stopped. He came to where I was and, nearly crying, he said, "I've just got to have a smoke." I told him God would help him and that he just needed to trust Him.

Henry kept saying, "I just gotta have a smoke!" In near desperation, he got on the ground and laid face-down on the overturned furrow and grasped the dirt with both hands.

He lay there a long time. I wondered if he had died.

All of a sudden he went pale and started weeping. I said, "What's wrong?" He stayed that way for quite a while without moving. I stood watching him, not quite sure what to make of it all. Eventually he started moving and then stood up with a smile on his face. "The battle is over," he stated matter-of-factly. "I don't want any more cigarettes. God has given me the victory and I am free!"

Some people seem to think that addictions are impossible to break, but with our Almighty God, nothing is impossible, as 1 Corinthians 10:13 tells us, "There hath no temptation taken you but such as is common to man: but God is faithful, who will not suffer you to be tempted above that ye are able; but will with the temptation also make a way to escape, that ye may be able to bear it." I witnessed God's power at work in Henry that day when he lost his urge to smoke.

Cheated Out of College Money

I was seventeen years old and I so badly wanted to attend college that I was often looking for ways to make and save money to pay for school. My parents promised that if I helped to get the crop in that year, they would give me a third of the profits to pay for school.

I worked hard and sometimes put in long hours. Many nights I worked until two in the morning. I really didn't mind though, because I had my sight fixed on college and the money I'd get from the crop would get me closer to my goal. Before I knew it, it was harvest time. We started harvesting the crop and when we were about two-thirds finished, my brother came home.

My mother loved Henry. It didn't seem to matter what he did, I believe my mother always treated him better than she treated me. After all the work I had put in on the farm, Mother came to me and said, "I can't pay you the money Dad and I promised you. Henry is the firstborn, and, therefore, he has more right to the money." I was terribly upset and felt as though I'd been cheated but there was nothing I could do about it.

Saved from Conscription by an Atomic Bomb

My family and I used to listen to the news every evening. It was 1944 and the allies had begun attacking Germany more forcefully. I was getting anxious because on August 9, 1945 I would turn eighteen. I knew that if I didn't enlist ahead of time, I would be conscripted. I wanted to be prepared because I wished to be a non-combatant. It was on August 6, 1945 that the US air force dropped a bomb on Hiroshima and on my eighteenth birthday, August 9, the second bomb was dropped on Nagasaki. It was on that day that Japan surrendered. Because of this, I didn't have to go to war.

End of the War

It was such a relief when the war ended. Everyone was celebrating. There was whooping and hollering in the streets. Grocers gave away candy and chocolate bars. There were no more ration coupons. We were again free to buy what we wanted and go where we wanted. It was wonderful to know that there would be no more war.

Nevertheless, there were positive outcomes because of the war. New friendships had been formed. During the war people worked together out of necessity and as a result of working together, we formed friendships with each other.

Only people who've experienced war can understand the terrible strain that it places on people, both those in active duty and those remaining on the home front. Only those who have lived through war times know the exhilaration at war's end.

A Well-earned Vacation

When Henry got my crop money, my dad felt so bad for me that he made me a deal to make up for it. He gave me the pig pasture and promised me that the following year if I put the crop in, worked it, and harvested it myself, I could have the profit and go for a holiday. It was only about an acre and a half but I worked it up really well and God blessed me. That piece of land produced better than any other place on the farm. It produced 90 bushels an acre! I sold the grain and went and bought a new pair of britches with a pretty yellow stripe down the side and a cap, something like the priests used to wear. I got on the bus and took off to Bassano to see my cousin, Benny.

When I arrived, Benny was being questioned by police because he was drunk and making trouble around town. He was arrested and brought to jail. I wasn't even allowed to visit him.

My efforts to see him thwarted, I went to my aunt's house. She was there crying about Benny and Rueben, her other son. She said, "I have nothing but trouble with my boys. They are irresponsible and always running in with the law."

I slept there that night and the next morning, not knowing how long Benny would be detained, I headed out on the bus to visit a cousin who lived in Calgary. When I got there, I stayed at her place. In those days, a trolley ticket cost twenty-five cents and you could ride all around town on the trolleys. I took a trolley to the zoo the first day and I don't recall what else I did while there. However, I soon tired of city life and after only a few days, I packed my bags and headed home. My trip did not last nearly as long as I had originally planned.

Cheated Again

When spring returned, Henry left home again. A second time Dad promised that if I worked with him to put the crop in, to care for it, and take it off in the fall, I would get a third of the harvest. He said, "This time I'll make sure you get the money." I loved my father and wanted to please him and I also needed the money so I agreed to work the farm with him again that year.

My father's health was failing. He had a heart attack while returning from a friend's funeral in Medicine Hat. Not wanting his condition to worsen, I tried to do more of the work around the farm so that he wouldn't have to. I worked very hard putting up the hay and completing all the other chores and duties that needed to be done. It was a dry year and, despite our efforts, the crop was poor. When harvest time came, I worked long hours bringing it in.

The crop had been harvested and I had delivered all but the last load to the elevator. Dad and I had just filled up the wagon and I was getting ready to drive into town with it, when Henry showed up. My heart sank at the sight of him.

Nervously, I continued on to Gadsby with the load in tow behind the tractor. I remember Fritze, my dog, keeping pace with me as I drove down the road. His crazy antics helped relieve my anxiety over my brother and whether or not my mother would give him the money which had been promised to me.

Suddenly, out jumped a rabbit. Fritze spotted it and before I could blink, the rabbit was off and Fritze was in hot pursuit. He chased the rabbit down the ditch and under the fence. The rabbit turned and streaked back toward the road. It ran under the wagon then under the tractor. I stopped the tractor to let Fritze at the rabbit and he chased it back into the field. He had nearly caught the rabbit when it doubled back a second time. A telephone pole stood between me and the rabbit. The rabbit bounded on what looked like a collision course with the pole. At the last moment it darted to the side. Fritze, unable to react quickly enough, ran headlong into the pole. The force caused his hind legs to fly over his body and his back crashed full length into the pole. Watching in horror, I heard the resounding crack and thud as his head and body slammed into the wood.

I ran to his lifeless body, picked him up, and ran back to the tractor with him. Working quickly, I unhooked the wagon and laid Fritze on one side of the tractor's platform. I drove home as fast as the tractor would go. My dad saw me coming back without the wagon and met me in the yard. I told him what had happened. He told me to sit on the dog while he grabbed Fritze by the head and pulled hard. Fritze's neck must have been dislocated because I heard a cracking sound and the dog immediately came to. I left Fritze with Dad and returned to the wagon to finish hauling the load to Gadsby. As I drove, I agonized over Fritze and worried that he was going to die. I loved him and wanted to get home as quickly as possible to be with him. I unloaded the grain, collected the payment and hurried home.[3]

When I got home Fritze was alive but listless. Dad told me, "I don't know if he's going to live." I prayed, "God, please heal my dog." Relieved that he was alive, I suddenly remembered my brother and I fretfully handed over the money to my dad. It didn't take long for Mother to tell me that Henry was again going to get the money that I had worked so hard for. Angrily, I fought terribly with her, but she stood firm. Resolutely she told me, "This will go my way whether you like it or not. Henry will get the third share of the crop. You're young. You can wait another year to go to school."

Infuriated but powerless, I ran away from home. My sister and brother-in-law lived

---

3   He was lying down, unable to lift his head. Dad said that he would probably die but I prayed often for him to recover and in time he did begin to lift his head. I just knew that God was answering my prayers. Nevertheless, by the time Fritze was running around, three months had passed.

about ten miles away so I went and stayed with them. A week later Dad arrived at my sister's place with Mom in tow. My mother apologized to me and admitted that she hadn't treated me right. I was glad to hear her say sorry but her apology didn't seem sincere. I later learned that my father had told her that if she didn't apologize to me, he would leave her. For my father's sake, I went home with my parents.

After I returned home, we prepared for our move to Stettler. We had an auction sale and immediately set about building our house in Stettler. It was a little house and was located along the highway. To this day it still stands there.

Henry had received my share of the money and by the time I came home from staying at my sister's, he had already left for Calgary. He didn't even stay home long enough to help out with the auction sale. He used the money to buy a Roadmaster Buick, the heaviest and biggest car made at that time. The rest of the money he wasted on drinking and partying at night. During the day he built houses for a company.

Logging Camp and Sickness

I couldn't attend college without money, so I went to work at Jack Houston's lumber camp, where my uncle Ted was already working. I became a lumberjack. After cutting a tree down, I would delimb it and cut it into proper lengths. I lived and worked at that camp all winter until springtime when I returned home.

One time while I was working at the camp, I got terribly sick. I started feeling rough on a Thursday and by Friday I was feeling even worse. My uncle Ted and the other guys I worked with asked if they could borrow my car and I told them they could as I wasn't feeling well and wouldn't be using it. So, on Friday afternoon they left with the car.

Left alone in the cabin, I only got sicker. My supply of firewood dwindled and then ran out. I hadn't the energy to cut more, so I lay shivering for hours until they returned on Sunday evening.

When they came in, I told them I wanted to go to the hospital. I was so weak and faint that I couldn't even stand properly, so they helped me out to my still-warm car and bade me off. I wanted to go to my parents' home in Stettler, about 130 miles (210 km) away. It was Sunday evening and the crew had to be at work first thing Monday morning, otherwise someone would have driven me home.

In those days top driving speed was 30 to 40 miles per hour (60 to 70 kilometres per hour). I drove for more than two hours and was just approaching Lacombe. As I drove the last few miles, it seemed to me that the road was weaving back and forth. I knew that I was too sick and tired to drive any farther so I stopped at a hotel in Lacombe, but there was no vacancy. The innkeeper, seeing my condition, said I could sleep in the lobby under the table. He even drained my radiator because I couldn't do it myself and he knew it would freeze if it wasn't drained.

All night I slept under a table beside a heat register. In the morning they filled my radiator with hot water and I determined to make it to Stettler that day. When I got there, I drove straight to the hospital. My temperature was 104 degrees and I was admitted immediately. At its peak, my temperature was 106 degrees and the nurses seemed to be continually changing my bed sheets as I kept soaking them from sweat. They kept putting ice on my head until my fever finally broke. After four or five days, when the fever peaked, I broke out in red spots. I had German measles. It was two weeks before I was finally well enough to leave the hospital. By the time I left the hospital it was nearly spring and I did not return to the logging camp.

Our Building Business

By the time I got out of the hospital, Henry had returned home. Armed with his house building experience and expertise, he talked Dad and me into starting up a home building business with him in Stettler. I had quite a bit of money saved from the work I had done in the logging camp. We purchased a number of city lots with my money and money Dad had saved from the previous fall's crop. For the remainder of the purchase price, we took out a loan with a bank. On credit I purchased a new Army Jeep that had not been used in the war effort for $750 which we used with a slip behind to dig the basements for the houses we built. The slip worked like a Fresno scraper, but it had two handles instead of one. After digging the basements and building the foundations, we built the houses and sold them.

We even built buildings other than houses. We built a tire shop for Mr. Jones and an apartment building for another man. With all that building, we were quite busy.

One day, Henry offered to buy the Jeep from me. I wanted to go to college in the fall so I agreed that he could have it if he made the payments on it. By that time, we had already built and sold maybe two or three houses. That very day, Henry took off with the Jeep. He didn't come back for nearly a week and Dad and I were wondering what had happened to him.

While away, he purchased some carpentry tools. Among them was a table saw, a planer and a time-punch clock. If memory serves me correctly, the clock cost him approximately $400. He showed it to me and said, "When you start work in the morning, I want you to punch the time onto a piece of paper and when you finish work in the evening, I want you to do the same."

"I have to punch the clock for you?" I asked in disbelief. "The only thing I'm going to punch is you!" and then I hit him on the side of the head. I knocked him right off the chair he was sitting on. Dad quickly got between the two of us and broke us up. I still had a lot to learn about meekness and humility in those days. God was very patient with me.

Not long after, we had an offer in Calgary, where my brother could be foreman and my dad could work in the shop. So, next spring we moved to Calgary and started working with Keith's Construction. I was hired as foreman for the floors and walls. My brother and Dad were in the shop building cabinets.

Chapter 5: Youth

Beginning to Work with God

Let him know, that he which converteth the sinner from the error of his way shall save a soul from death, and shall hide a multitude of sins. James 5:20

One day I heard one of the construction workers singing and humming songs that sounded familiar to me. He had a cigarette in his mouth, but he was humming old-fashioned Adventist songs. I recognized the songs and could even sing some of them in German. I went to him and asked, "Do you go to church? Are you an Adventist by chance?" He said, "I was raised an Adventist, but I don't go to church anymore." I told him, "You know, you should. I can tell on your face that you're missing something. You're not happy." We talked quite a bit after that. It wasn't long before he said, "Ben, I'm going to go back to church." And he did. He was my first convert. I felt really blessed about telling him to go back to church and I thanked God for that opportunity.

Miraculously Spared Serious Injury

Just before I went to college I was trying to make some extra money. I went to Rocky Mountain house to dig up some spruce trees. I took a truckload to Hanna and unloaded them. I thought if I hurried, I could get another load and take it to Stettler. I was driving along at 60 miles per hour (100 km/hour) on the gravel road and a vehicle went by. I put my hand up to my face. I had no reason to do that, but the Lord was protecting me. Just as the vehicle passed, a stone hit my windshield. Of all things, that windshield wasn't made of shatterproof glass! Every part of my face that wasn't covered by my hand was cut and bleeding and so was my hand. If just one of those little pieces of glass had gotten into one of my eyes, it would have cut my eye.

Another driver stopped and took me to the hospital where the doctors pulled out the glass bits and wrapped my hand. The good Lord protected me. I never even saw the rock and wouldn't have had time to put my hand up even if I had. I was sure thankful for God's protection.

Chapter 6: Bittersweet College Days

In the fall of 1946, I was finally going to college. Myrna, David, Herb, Fergie, and I would all be attending school together, so a week before school began we loaded my car up with as much of our belongings as could fit in the car. We all piled into the car and I drove them up to the house we would be renting in Rosedale Valley. David and Fergie's mom, Stella, would stay with us and cook for us. After we got ourselves situated, our first year of college was wonderful. We enjoyed our time together very much.

God's Gifts: A Mitt and a Caboose Ride

I used to hitchhike home to Stettler some weekends to see my parents. I saved money by hitchhiking rather than driving my own car. One weekend late that first fall I was on the road and a couple from California picked me up in a Chrysler New Yorker. We drove a few miles and the man asked me, "Can you drive a car?"

"I've driven lots and made half a million miles by now," I told him proudly.

He said, "Well, I'd really appreciate if you'd drive."

So I changed places with him and took the steering wheel. The little girl came into the front and her parents got in the back seat for a little rest. They were on their way home to California.

Then it started to snow. Well, they had never seen snow in their lives, because they lived in southern California. They were so excited that I had to stop the car for them to get out.

"This is not so wonderful if you have to shovel it and get stuck in it and it's 20 below," I told them.

When we got to Stettler, the man told me they wanted to continue on to Drumheller.

"I wish you could have driven my car farther," he said, as I pulled up along the curb in front of my parents' house.

Quickly, I decided this was an opportunity for me to do something different, so I said, "I'll tell you what. I'll drive you to Drumheller and visit with my sister and brother-in-law who live there."

We went to a café in Drumheller and had a bite to eat and they paid for my meal. The man told me, "Visiting with you has been the highlight of our trip." We said our goodbyes and I spent some time with my sister.

Sunday morning I headed back to college. I walked up the steep hill that leads out of the valley where the town sits and had gone about two miles when it started to snow. There were little pieces of ice mixed with the snow and I was completely unprepared for being out in that weather. I had no gloves and had just a little suitcase with me. I'd carry it with one hand and keep the other hand in my pocket then I'd change hands. I started wishing I had just one mitt.

I walked along a little way and saw something black lying on the side of the road and walked up to it. It was a mitt. I put it on and carried my suitcase in my mittened hand. A couple of miles farther along, I caught up to a train. It was just picking up speed after leaving Drumheller. The engineer looked out of the engine window, back along the side of the train and saw me coming along on the road. Then the train started slowing down, though there was no town in sight. I caught up with the caboose at the back of the train and a man came out the back of it. He called to me, "Do you want a ride?"

Have you ever had a train stop to ask you if you wanted a ride? It just doesn't happen. The good Lord has been so good to me! The things you could never imagine happening show how much God loves us. We have to always remember that.

The Tall House

I decided to buy a house so my friends and I wouldn't have to pay rent for the next few years. In the long run, it would save us money and I would be able to sell it when we finished college. That summer, David and I went looking for a house. We spent some hours driving around, searching. Then David spotted one that was located seven miles north of the college.

It was a two-storey house with plastered interior walls. The exterior was board siding. If I bought it, we'd have to transport it from its location to somewhere near the college. There was a bare lot for sale in Rosedale Valley. I purchased the house for $125 which would be approximately $12,500 today and the lot for $400 (about $40,000 today).

After that, the real work began. David and Fergie agreed to help me move the house. My brother Henry and I had a house moving business in the Stettler area and we used an Army-Gunn Tractor to pull the houses. We used that tractor to move the house I had purchased.

Our first task was to raise the house with jacks. It was sitting flat on the ground and in order to get the jacks under it, we had to dig holes beneath it. After the holes had been dug and the jacks positioned, we raised one jack a little then another. Then, we'd move to the next one until we had raised all of them. Because the jacks could only lift six inches at a time, we would then block each one and begin the process all over again. As we worked, the house creaked and groaned because it was being twisted each time we hoisted a jack. The ground was soft and sandy and the jacks sank into the soil. The day was drawing to a close and the lifting of the house—a job which should have only taken a day to complete—was nowhere near being finished. I began to think that I might have bitten off more than I could chew, so to speak. But, by that time, it was too late. I had already purchased the house—the papers were signed—it was a done deal.

We worked right until dark before turning in for the night. The house didn't have a front door but it did have a roof which made it better than sleeping outside. We had brought a box spring and mattress with us to sleep on. We had just lain down and turned off the gas lantern when we began hearing a rustling in the bushes just outside. Whatever it was seemed to be coming straight toward the house because the noise just kept getting louder. We worried that a bear or some other wild animal would wander through the open door right into the house.

Suddenly, there was a loud noise and a large section of plaster fell off the ceiling and landed on the bed. The plaster had been twisted numerous times throughout the day as we jacked the house and had cracked in several places, compromising its strength. We weren't aware of this until it fell on us. We sprang out of bed and shook off all the plaster that had fallen on the sheets. After that, we didn't hear the rustling from outside again.

The next morning we went around the house breaking off any sections of plaster that had worked loose the day before. It was while we were doing this that I realized that between the plastered interior walls and the exterior board siding there were solid logs. What looked like a framed house was actually a log house. I understood then why the jacks had kept sinking into the sand.

Early next morning we went back to work on the house. By the time the house had been raised high enough for us to move it, nearly three whole days had passed since we'd started. To move houses, we used a rather interesting contraption. This consisted of a steel beam called a bunker which was attached to the back of the tractor in the center of the beam by a pin that allowed the bunker to pivot. Attached to the tractor at either end of the bunker were two logs, each 70 feet long[1]. Attached to the back end of each log were two dollies[2]. The college was only seven miles away. The tractor could go about five miles per hour, so we didn't expect it to take very long to get it to Rosedale Valley.

The Army-Gunn tractor was excellent for moving houses because we could gear it down very low and literally inch along with it. Even if the road was bumpy, the tractor moved so slowly that the house would not be jostled. Some of the houses we'd moved still had the furniture set out in it and a couple of times, we even moved the houses while the owners were still inside.

Because of the extreme weight of the house, we had to gear the tractor down so much that we were in danger of tearing out the differential gear[3] of the tractor. The dollies had sunk into the ground after we'd placed the house on the logs. I knew it would be difficult to start moving the house. The tractor tried to pull the load but under the weight of the house, the tractor tires and the dollies had sunk so deep into the soft, sandy ground that it was nearly impossible. The tractor worked so hard that the crown gear and the pinion got stripped and stopped working altogether. The house had barely budged and the job was already halted.

---

1   These were power line poles we had purchased from the power company (CalGary Power at that time).
2   Truck wheels
3   An epicyclic (a circle whose circumference rolls along the circumference of a fixed circle) train of gears designed to permit two or more shafts to rotate at different speeds, as a set of gears in an automobile permitting the rear wheels to be driven at different speeds when it is turning.

We took a trip into Stettler to the armoury to get a replacement differential. A few hours later, we had replaced the differential and we were ready to get at it again. This time we jacked up the logs and placed boards under the wheels. We had no trouble moving the house then and we were finally on our way.

We pulled the tractor and house slowly up the hill on what is now the 58th Street extension just outside of Rosedale Valley and overlooking Lake Barnett. Fergie walked ahead of me to make sure that I didn't catch the bank on the left side with the house. Our excitement was mounting—we had nearly reached our destination.

Part way up the hill, the tractor just stopped moving. Without Fergie seeing, the house had hit the bank and after it had dragged about 20 feet of dirt along with it, the tractor reached its breaking point again. We backed down the hill far enough to stop the house from touching the bank. After that we could do nothing but leave the tractor and the house right where they sat. The house, took up the whole road and anyone travelling on it had to turn around and take an alternate route. It sat there the rest of the day and the entire night. The next morning we replaced the differential again and arrived at the lot. At the lot, we had to negotiate almost a complete turn of 360 degrees, which was very difficult. However, after some time we did get the job done and were able to place the house in its new location. That house still sits where we put it. It is the first house on the left entering Rosedale Valley from 58th Street. The house became known as the Tall House. I guess we called it that for two reasons. At that time, because it was two-stories, it was the tallest house on campus and, incidentally, I had purchased it from a man named Mr. Tall.

The College Money Heist

Although I had purchased the Tall House and moved it to Rosedale Valley, it still wasn't in liveable condition. The interior plaster needed to be repaired and painted, the front door needed to be installed, and there were numerous other minor repairs which needed to be finished. I went back home to work for the summer and raise money for school the following year and left the house as it was with the commitment that I would return and work on it in my spare time after returning to school in the fall.

I joined my dad and brother who were still building houses. All summer I worked with them and by summer's end, I had saved about $1100 for college expenses. It was time for me to leave and Henry took off on a trip. Dad and I didn't know where he was or what he was doing. All my stuff was packed in my little car. Before leaving town, I stopped at the bank to withdraw the money from the account that I shared with Henry and my dad. But the money was gone. Henry had withdrawn all the money from the account. I later learned that true to his form, he had spent the entire sum getting drunk.

Frantically, I stayed back from school to work for Mr. Anderson making as much money as I could. He paid by the hour. I ran his brand new combine and pretty near worked all day and night until the crop was either finished or too wet to harvest. I'm not sure if I even changed my clothes during those days.

I took a day off from working at Mr. Anderson's farm to help get Fergie, Herb and

Myrna get settled in the house at College Heights. Then, I returned to Mr. Anderson's farm to continue with harvest. During the month I worked for him, I sold the Tall House and my friends moved into a rental house.

I started school about five weeks late. The teachers were concerned I wouldn't be able to catch up. The French teacher even scolded me in front of the class. However, I worked hard and eventually did get caught up. I learned French quickly because it came to me easily. The French teacher used my work for an example to motivate the rest of the class when others were having trouble learning. She told them, "If he came in late and could do it, then you can do it, too."

The Washing Machine Motor Fiasco

While I was working at Mr. Anderson's farm, a chain of events was set in motion which would eventually prove to forever alter the course of our lives. It started out small and innocently enough, though.

In the yard of the house we were renting sat an old washing machine. Judging from its condition, it had lain there for years. At one time or another, someone had removed its engine and it too had clearly sat there on the grass beside the washing machine for years.

One day, Fergie, the youngest member of our group, got the notion that he'd like to have the old motor to tinker around with. He discussed this with our landlord's son and he sold it to Fergie for four dollars. Fergie worked with it but could not get it to run. He sold it to David who also could not get it running. Eventually David sold it to me. I don't recall paying him for it but we were always trading things on account of a lack of money, so I must have given him something in exchange for it.

Eventually, I got the motor running. I painted it black and it looked shiny and new. I took it to Marshall Wells, the hardware store, and got $29 for it. As we didn't often have enough money for groceries, this money was truly a blessing.

One day, not long afterward, the college president called the four of us boys to his office. While we had been in class, the president had been visited by police officers, he told us. They told him that our landlord had reported us as having stolen a washing machine motor from her yard and then selling it to the hardware store. She must not have known about the arrangement made between her son and Fergie.

The president explained to us that any student responsible for bringing the police to the school would automatically be expelled. So, he expelled us. We were stunned! Myrna and Herb had not even been involved in the situation except that they lived in the same house with Fergie, Dave, and me. The president expelled all of us.

We tried to reason with the president and told him our side of the story but it made no difference. He stood firmly by his decision. When our teachers realized what had happened, they stood up for us. We could hear them arguing with the president outside the president's office, but he would not relent.

Seeing that there was nothing to be done, Myrna, Herb, David, and Fergie packed their things and returned home, but I was determined to finish college. One of the teachers even fought for my right to continue. The president was unbending. He made it clear that I would receive no credit for the classes I was attending. With the encouragement of some of my teachers, I decided to stick it out right up until the end of the school year in hopes that he might change his mind. I worked hard. I completed my assignments and wrote exams just like everyone else, but the president told me that I wouldn't get credits for any of my classes. I tried to go on as I had before, but I felt really discouraged.

Chapter 7: Heartbreak

James 3:5 says, "Behold, How great a matter a little fire kindleth!" This verse aptly describes the events that began unfolding in the Erskine church around the same time that my friends and I had been expelled from school.

I loved Mr. Anderson. He was the kind of man everyone wants to have as a friend. He was financially successful but also such a kind and generous man and he was well known by the church members for his success and fine character traits.

One family asked Mr. Anderson if he would please lend them $50 to purchase binder twine so they could bale their crop. Mr. Anderson agreed to lend them the money. Shortly after, another family, new converts to the church and poorer even than the first also asked Mr. Anderson for money to buy binder twine for baling. I don't understand why, but, to this family, he said no. His decision caused quite a stir in the church.

Myrna and Herb's family had been good friends of this second family. Mr. Erickson, Myrna's father, was incensed. It was all just too much for him to bear what with Myrna and Herb getting expelled for no fault of their own and Mr. Anderson refusing to lend money to his friends. Myrna and Herb's parents came to the conclusion that if this was the way Seventh-day Adventists treated each other, they wanted no part of the church. They immediately stopped attending church and associating with it. David and Fergie's parents also cut ties with the church. It wasn't long before Myrna, Herb, David, and Fergie stopped attending church also.

It didn't take long for what had been a growing church to be reduced to two older families and no hope for growth. Not long after that, the church closed its doors

Heartbreak and Breakup

One Saturday evening shortly after this, I went out to Myrna's family's farm. I could tell by the sounds coming from the barn that a party was in full swing. Silently I peeked up through the steps to see what was going on. Mr. Erickson was playing "Turkey in the Straw" on the fiddle. I could also hear saxophones and an accordion and perhaps there were other instruments as well. The music was lively and I could see that everyone there was having a great time laughing and dancing. I ducked down the stairs as quietly as I had come and left without anyone seeing me. I was crying—my spirit crushed. In fact, I cried all the way home.

A few weeks later, after giving much thought to what was happening, I broke off my engagement with Myrna. As we had been a couple for three years and earnestly planning to be married, it was a difficult and painful decision for me to make. Myrna emphatically replied, "You can't break up with me. You are going to marry me!" I told her that if she wasn't going to live right and come to church anymore, I could no longer be in a relationship with her.

The President Apologizes

During the spring of that year, the school had planned a week of prayer. It was to be a time of spiritual reawakening. At some point during that week, I met the college president in the stairwell. He was on his way up as I was on my way down. He said he wished to talk to me, but I resisted. In fact, he'd tried to stop me several times before and I had always managed to avoid him successfully. This time he stopped me and apologized for expelling me and my friends.

Perhaps the spiritual atmosphere created by the week of prayer had put him under conviction. I've never really understood why he apologized to me then. But I was angry at the college president and I didn't care for his apology at that time. I only saw him as the reason for all the horrible things that were happening in my life. I had lost my fiancée and my friends. I had even lost my opportunity to obtain a college education and I held him responsible for all of that. I told him that his apology was meaningless to me and tried to explain to him that his actions had directly influenced all of the others and their families to leave the church. I told him that the happiness in my life was gone because of him and that he would be held accountable for his part in the eternal loss of two families.[1]

After my outburst, the college president started crying. I could tell that he felt deeply sorry for his actions and the consequences that had been wrought as a result of them. I had already been crying from frustration and anger, but the sight of genuine sorrow on this man's face caused my heart to soften and I felt bad for myself and for him. Before I knew it we were both crying from sadness and although we had met as enemies, at least in my mind, we parted as friends.

Voices of Angels

My reconciliation with the college president encouraged me temporarily, but it wasn't long before discouragement and despair threatened to overtake me again. I thought constantly about my friends, especially Myrna. I wasn't able to sleep properly at night. Because I was tired and also because I was heartbroken, I couldn't concentrate in class, I was unable to study, and I couldn't remember anything I managed to work on. I went to the doctor because I felt as though my life was falling apart. He counselled me to quit attending classes and go home to relax because, as he said, I really would fall apart if I continued. "You have been under too much mental strain. If you don't stop, you will likely have a complete mental breakdown," he told me.

Becoming a preacher had been the foremost goal of my life and although I'd been

---

[1] Despite my anger at that time we were later able to become friends and after I got married, my wife and I stayed at their home in Walla Walla, Washington for a portion of our honeymoon.

barely hanging on to that goal, at the time I had felt as though it was the only thing I had left to live for. I went home in such despair that I felt as though I could never be happy again. I slumped to the floor by my bed and poured out a most pathetic prayer. "God," I groaned, "I just can't take this anymore. I'm not allowed to finish school, the only best friends I ever had are gone, and my girlfriend is gone. I ache like everything. I have nothing left to live for and I just can't bear it any longer." Immobilized by my emotional pain, I stayed on the floor that way for a while. I was tempted to leave God and the church, embrace the world, and return to Myrna. I wrestled with this temptation as I knelt on the floor.

The load on my chest was so heavy I thought my chest would collapse. It hurt so much I was afraid I might even have a heart attack. It seems a funny thing to me now but I didn't want to live, yet I didn't want to die either. It was then that I heard singing that sounded as though it was coming from a chorus up in the air just outside the house. "Oh weary soul, the gate is near, in sin why still abide? Both peace and rest are waiting here and you are just outside," sang the mysterious voices. The song continued and after hearing it, I had the courage to carry on. I'm sure the song I heard had been sung by angels. Again, God impressed upon my mind that He still loved me and if I remained faithful to Him rather than following the ways of sin, I had the promise of heaven and eternal life with Him to look forward to. I decided to take Dr. Tetz's advice. I packed up just before the end of the school year and went home for good.

Caretaking Mr. Anderson's Farm

Shortly after I stopped attending classes, Mr. Anderson wanted to take a trip down to Sacramento, California. Most of his family members lived there and it had been quite some time since he had visited them. He figured it would take about four weeks for him to make the trip there and back. In those days, automobiles didn't drive as fast as they do now, flat tires and overheated vehicles were a common occurrence, and there were numerous other possible causes for which one might have to stop and wait on the roadside for a time.

Mr. Anderson asked me if I would look after his farm while he was gone. I'd have summer fallowing to do and, when harvest time came, crop swathing. After the swathing, the land would need tilling. He knew I was capable enough to handle the responsibility of doing this. I knew he trusted me because he had even gotten me to purchase equipment for him once. I told Mr. Anderson that I would be happy to care for his farm.

Once Mr. and Mrs. Anderson had gone, I suddenly realized how alone I was. The nearest town was Stettler, ten miles away. There was plenty to do though, so I didn't think about being alone for very long. All week I kept myself busy doing my chores, but on Friday afternoon, as the Sabbath neared, the pain and hurt came flooding back to me as I thought of Myrna and my friends and what I'd lost with them. I went to church the next morning and there were just a few of the older folks sitting in the front pews. Other than the times I was needed up front to play the piano during the service, I sat in the back row heartsick and lonely, trying to keep from crying. After the service, I returned to the Anderson farm and vowed, "Next Sabbath, I will not go to church!"

A Small Rain Cloud and a Rolophone

The following week, I busied myself with my duties but as Friday evening approached my thoughts again turned toward my friends and Myrna and my heart began aching again. I felt that the pain of going to church the next day and being there alone without my friends would be too much for me to bear.

I was tilling. The shining sun was beginning to dip in the clear sky. As I approached an old granary in the middle of the field, a small white cloud appeared above me, seemingly from nowhere, and began to sprinkle on me. I was already dispirited and the light shower did nothing to cheer me. The rain intensified and I couldn't figure how so much moisture could fit into such a small cloud. There was no cab on the tractor so I stopped it, shut it off, hopped off, and went into the granary to keep dry.

Once inside, I noticed the shingles were still intact on one half of the roof while the other half had been stripped of shingles down to the bare boards. I could see the sky above. There was an old cylinder phonograph[2] sitting on the floor inside the granary. Under a layer of dust, an old record[3] was still in place around the tumbler. I wound up the player and blew the dust off. I helped it along at first but it was spinning.

Out played the words, "Master, the tempest is raging. The billows are tossing high." And there I stood with my raging heart which had been tossed, turned, and torn apart by waves of despair and despondency. I felt so mixed up and broken. I just knew that God must have placed that gramophone there some time in the past so that it would be there at the very moment I needed it most. Weeping, I fell to my knees asking God to forgive me for not wanting to go to church. I listened to the rest of the record and the song, "Jesus, Lover of my Soul" was also on it.

I went to church in the morning. Playing the piano was the only break I got from the overwhelming grief of missing my friends. It was pure agony for me to sit in the back pew by myself. I felt so all alone and the pain was all but unbearable. After church let out, I returned to the Anderson's cried most of the way back to the farm. Again I made a firm decision not to go back to church the following Sabbath. I would not give up on God, but I no longer wished to attend church if I was going to have to go and be there alone.

My Golden-Haired Cherub

While I busied myself about my chores the next week, the pain in my heart subsided, but around rolled Friday again. Inevitably, my thoughts began to wander to Myrna and

---

2   The cylinder phonograph/gramophone was the predecessor to the more commonly known flat phonograph/gramophone. It was a tubular shaped tumbler. The records were sleeve shaped and fitted over the tumbler.
3   This particular record had been recorded by Homer Alvan Rodeheaver (October 4, 1880—December 18, 1955) who was an American evangelist, music director, music publisher, composer of gospel songs, and pioneer in the recording of sacred music.

the friendships I had lost with her, her brother, and cousins. I was given to bouts of crying each time I thought of the hopelessness of my situation.

This time I was swathing and I spotted what appeared to be a little golden-haired girl walking towards me through the grain. Her hair matched the colour of the grain and I began to wonder if she was just a figment of my imagination or possibly even an angel. But she was neither.

Hopping and skipping she came right up to me and asked, "Can I have a ride on your tractor?" She couldn't have been more than six or seven years of age. I invited her up onto the tractor and asked her where she had come from, for I thought she must be an angel. She pointed and answered, "Oh, I just live about a mile that way."

She told me that her family was staying in a motor home on a piece of land not far from where we were. She was an oilfield worker's daughter. I later realized that from a half-mile away she had seen me driving the tractor around in the field. I told her that since there was no place to stand on this tractor she would have to sit on my knee.

"That's okay," she said. So she climbed up, sat on my knee, put her arms around my neck, and off we went. She was so friendly, so lively, and so sweet. I just knew God had sent her to cheer my spirits.

I told her that I couldn't work much longer because the sun would soon be going down. I added, "The Sabbath starts at sundown and I don't do any work on the Sabbath."

"Oh no," she solemnly declared, "Sunday is the day to go to church." She said her family was Pentecostal and her mother was even a Bible teacher. After finishing my work, she followed me to the house and I showed her in the Bible all the verses which talked about the Sabbath.[4]

She asked me, "Could I take this Bible to my mommy?" I told her yes but made sure that she promised to bring my Bible back to me. I offered to drive her home but she said, "No, I'll just run across the field," and she slipped through the wheat just the same way as she had come. Her golden hair bobbed as she went and then she disappeared from my sight.

She was such a sweetheart and I was sure that the Lord had used her to speak to me so I went to church the following day.

I didn't see "my golden-haired cherub" again until two years later. After helping Mr. Anderson build a house in town, we built a number of shacks for oilfield workers. While building the shacks I saw that little girl and not knowing her name, I asked, "Hey, little girl where's my Bible? You never brought it back to me." She said, "Oh, my mother burned it. She said all Adventist Bibles should be burned."

I replied, "That Bible was no more Adventist than any other Bible, it was the same as other Bibles." "Mother said it was an Adventist Bible," she said resolutely. I asked her to take me to her mother. She led me to the trailer they lived in. She opened the door and introduced me to her mother as the man who had given her "that" Bible.

Immediately her mother began to denounce me angrily and question how I could have

---

4   I had previously marked these texts with red ink.

given an Adventist Bible to her daughter.

"Adventist Bibles should all be destroyed and, for that matter, so should the Adventists," she said emphatically.

"Why?" I asked, incredulous that she was so angry.

"All that Saturday business in your Bible… well, it just isn't right," she continued.

"What kind of Bible do you read?" I asked her.

"We use the King James Bible," she told me.

"My Bible, the one you burned, was a King James Bible."

"No it wasn't, young man," she insisted. "I know what I read!"

Then I said to her, "The Lord says in Matthew 13:13, 14 and Mark 8:18, that although we have eyes and ears we do not see or hear, remember or understand."

"I'll show you," she said and went to her bedroom to fetch her Bible. When she returned, I opened up her Bible to Genesis chapter 2 and read to her what it said about the Sabbath. I noticed her face redden as I read the words. I jumped to Exodus chapter 20 and Deuteronomy 5.

"I never knew that," she said. "I never knew that it was the same Bible. I always thought that the Sabbath references were added by Adventists. I'm going to pay you for the Bible I destroyed."

She offered me $15.00 (which was quite a lot of money at that time) but I refused her money. I told her that I already had another Bible and that she didn't need to pay for it. I did tell her that I hoped she'd follow the Bible. She said she would but I never saw her again after that. This all happened two years after I quit attending college.

A Drunken Cure?

Meanwhile as I continued looking after Mr. Anderson's, I still ached over Myrna. The week flew by again and the Friday sun had set, ushering in the Sabbath. My heart weighed heavy. My sister, Lillian, and brother-in-law, Albert, had gotten directions to where I was staying from my mother in Stettler. I wasn't expecting them and by the time they arrived, my spirits were so low that I don't think they could have gotten any lower. My sister and Albert could see that I was hurting.

They said to me, "Why don't you come over to Endiang? We're having a dance tonight. You can get drunk and forget your troubles." My sisters were not opposed to getting drunk and my brother was an alcoholic. Wanting to numb the pain of my hurting heart, I decided to go to the dance that night and not go to church the following day.

I fully intended to get drunk that night. I wasn't interested in having fun but I wanted my problems to go away. There was a restless, uneasy feeling in the pit of my stomach, but I dismissed it. The Holy Spirit was calling me back, but all I wanted was to forget my aching heart, if only for one night.

I arrived and went into the hall. Albert opened a bottle of beer and handed it to me. I'd never tasted beer before. Swallowing the nervous feeling in my core, I determined to drink it even if it tasted awful.

I put the bottle to my mouth but could not take even a sip. After willing myself to drink the beer a number of times and being unable to do so, it became clear to me that God was withholding me from drinking it. I passed the bottle back to Albert and ran out of the hall and into the car. Weeping bitterly, I prayed, "God, I'm sorry for wanting to get drunk. Please forgive me."

So, again I went to church, sat in the back, and went home feeling hollow and empty inside. On my way home, I promised myself the third time that I would not go to church the following week.

My Walking Companion

It was that next week that the Andersons returned. They asked me to go to church with them. I wanted to say no, but I didn't have the nerve because I really did love them. After all, they had always been so good to me. I also still had hope that at least one of my friends would be there, but none of them were. My hopes dashed again, I sat in the back corner while Mrs. Anderson played the piano and the congregation sang the opening song, "Be silent, be silent, a whisper is heard." There were only two families there and their old voices seemed to dig at the very core of my being. As I heard the words, "He bids us draw near," I couldn't take it anymore.

The room began to close in on me and I felt as though I couldn't breathe. I bolted and ran from the church. Mr. Anderson came to the door and called after me to come back but I just kept on running. I went across the highway, over the railway track, between the grain elevators, over a fence, and into a farmer's field, running the whole way. I later discovered that I had run eight miles.

After coming to myself, my eyes still blurred with tears, I didn't know where I was. I was walking along a sandy road I didn't recognize. Suddenly, I heard footsteps behind me. Startled, I turned around quickly but there wasn't anything or anyone there. I started walking again. I was watching on the left side of me while walking on the slanted edge of the left side of the road. I could see footprints walking in the sand, but no feet. I thought it might be Jesus or an angel so I moved over so that He, or whoever it was, wouldn't have to walk in the ditch. There was an intersection just a little distance away. I walked to the intersection and I just knew that God was doing something. When I reached the crossroads, I knelt and bowed my head low to the ground. My face was between my knees, my nose in the sand.

I was weeping. Then I heard singing. There wasn't a single soul anywhere near me. It could only have been the voices of angels that I heard that day. The song they sang was, "Take Up Thy Cross and Follow Me," a song by Alfred Henry Ackley

Chapter 7: Heartbreak

<h2 style="text-align:center">Take Up Thy Cross and Follow Me
by Alfred Henry Ackley (1887-1960)—1922</h2>

*I walked one day along a country road,/ And there a stranger journeyed too,
Bent low beneath the burned of His load:/ It was a cross, a cross I knew.*

*Chorus:
"Take up the cross and follow Me,"/ I hear the blessed Savior call;
How can I make a lesser sacrifice,/ When Jesus gave His all?*

*I cried, "Lord Jesus," and He spoke my name;/ I saw His hands all bruised and torn;
I stooped to kiss away the marks of shame,/ The shame for me that He had borne.*

Chorus

*"Oh, let me bear Thy cross, dear Lord," I cried,/ And, lo, a cross for me appeared,
The one, forgotten, I had cast aside,/ The one, so long, that I had feared.*

Chorus

*My cross I'll carry till the crown appears/ The way I journey soon will end
Where God Himself shall wipe away all tears,/ And friend hold fellowship with friend.*

The awful weight of the burdens I'd been carrying for so long was lifted from me at that very moment.

After the indescribably beautiful singing stopped, I still didn't know where I was but I continued walking, and eventually I began to recognize my surroundings. I made my way back to the Anderson farm. The following week the church board met and decided to close down the church.

More Heartbreak and Forsaken Hope

I still missed Myrna and my friends. I had spent so much time at their place before that it was almost as though I lived there. I wanted to see them again and wished that they would come back to church so I decided to go out to their place to see if I could talk to them about the Sabbath and persuade them to come back to church. I parked down the road from the farm and walked the rest of the way so that no one would know I was there. As I neared the yard, I could see the lights in the barn and hear the sound of music filtering down just like the time I had been there before. I snuck up the stairs the same way I had the last time.

This time I saw Myrna dancing with a boy I didn't recognize and the sight of her in someone else's arms cut straight to my heart as though a knife had been plunged deeply into me. Herb and David were also dancing with young ladies and beer bottles littered the floor. Turning quietly, I went down the stairs and left in despair.

After that I went to our favourite bush. In happier times we had gone there to pray together. It was a beautiful evening and I looked up at the full and bright easterly moon. I felt completely alone. I dropped to my knees. So many families had left the church that it had had to close its doors. I cried out for God to help me. While I was praying, I heard a car drive up and stop near where I was.

After a little while, I heard footsteps. Apparently someone had spotted me at the barn, so David, Fergie, Herb, and Myrna had left their party to come and find me. They figured I would be at our special prayer spot, and they were right. They knelt around me and I told them I was hurting so bad that I'd just like to die. They said, "Ben, we'll come back to church again soon. Just give us a little time." We cried on one another's shoulders and I felt better. That night I fell asleep with hope in my heart that they would indeed return to church.

The following Friday I was anxious. They had not spoken of a recommitment to Christ and I feared they had just said what I wanted to hear to make me feel better. I feared they would not come again as they had said they would. Sabbath morning they were not in church and my heart broke again.

In the following weeks I waited for them to come back to church, but, week after week, when they did not return I began to realize they never would. I knew that God loved me and although I felt my heart breaking, I was able to resist the despair that threatened to overwhelm me. For a long time, Friday evenings and Sabbaths were the hardest days of each week. Healing took a very long time as each weekend brought back the pain and battered me like fresh, hard waves.

David's Return

Only a few weeks later, David came to me and said that he wanted to come back to God. He had taken up with a woman twenty years his senior and after they'd been together a number of weeks, she confessed that she was pregnant by him. Trying to be honourable and do the right thing, he married her quickly.

By the time he came to see me, he was already married. Feeling the enormous pressure of becoming a father, he wanted to return to a life of faith and trust in God so that he'd be able to raise his child properly. We prayed together and he recommitted his life to Christ. David later learned that the child wasn't his. Nevertheless, he remained faithful to God and to his wife.

A few years later he contracted throat cancer and died shortly afterward. To the end, he remained firmly committed to God and I look forward to seeing him again in heaven.

Herb's Return

David's conversion encouraged me and I began writing letters to Herb on a consistent basis and even visited him several times in Edmonton.

One time when I visited, he was drunk. That evening he'd lost not only his hat and keys, but also his car. He was all messed up, so I helped clean him up. I prayed for him and then he said, "Ben, would you pull out that dresser drawer for me?"

Inside the drawer were all the letters I had written to him over a number of years.

"Ben," he said, "Keep writing. I want to come back to God."

I always told him, "Herb, when I get to Heaven, I don't want to have to look all over Heaven for you. I'd like to sing with you again, that song we used to sing, Love divine! Oh sing the wondrous story; far and near the glorious news proclaim." He always used to tell me, "Ben, I'm going to come back. I'll come back." But it was years before he did.

Maybe it was thirty years later, Shirley and I were on the way home from Two Hills where we were visiting Shirley's father. The Lord must have stopped my watch deliberately, because I didn't know it was late. I told Shirley, "I'm going to find Herb. He's out at St. Albert." That was on our way home.

She said, "Oh, Ben, don't stop this late. We don't want to call on him this late at night." We didn't know who his wife was. He was on his third wife already. But I said, "No, I'm going to find him. I want to see him."

We stopped at a service station and found his phone number and called him. He was glad to hear from me and invited us to come over. Shirley said, "It's awfully late." I didn't know my watch had stopped, I think it said 8 p.m., but it turned out to be 10. When we got there, we met his wife, Carol. We talked about good times. He said the best time of his life was when we spent time together and when we used to go to church together. He said he wished it was like that again. I gave him *Desire of Ages*.

Six or eight months later, they came out to see us. Again, I told him, "Herb, I don't want to hunt all over Heaven for you. I want to sing with you *Love Divine* again."

He said, "That's why we're here. Carol and I have been studying and reading that book, *Desire of Ages*. It's changed my whole life. I quit smoking. I quit drinking. We want to be Christians and join the church again."

I cried, I was so happy. I said, "Thank God!" They returned home with plans to be baptized.

Only two or three nights later, he had a heart attack and died. I really believe that I'll see him in the kingdom, though, because he had made up his mind to be baptized and start all over again.

A Wrecked Record and Forgetting

Not long after David's conversion, my parents moved to Calgary and I went with them. During the time that Myrna and I had been together, she had made a record for me of a song called, "God Understands." After moving to Calgary, I continued to miss Myrna as much as I ever had and perhaps even more. I played that record whenever I thought of her and I rarely stopped thinking of her. In fact, I played the record so much that the outer layer literally peeled right off. Yet, no matter how much I missed her, I wouldn't take her back unless she turned her life around and pledged herself to God and living right again.

Once her record fell apart, I made efforts to forget her. My parents attended the Bridgeland SDA Church while I attended the Calgary Central SDA Church. At that time, there were more young people attending the Central Church and I wanted to be around people my age. I started building friendships with a number of the young people who regularly attended there. Many times a bunch of us young people took trips out to Banff and other places. And so my heart began to slowly heal.

Chapter 8: New Beginnings

He that is surety for a stranger shall smart for it: and he that hateth suretiship is sure. Proverbs 11:15

During the time Dad and Henry and I had our construction company, we built two eight-suite apartment buildings for a man. The buildings were on his property and we depleted our savings and even used credit when the savings ran out to buy the building materials. We had sold the cattle, the farm and the machinery to pay for the building materials. We worked hard and the inspectors complimented us on the fine job we had done and told us that if every builder completed their jobs as well as we had, there wouldn't be any need for inspectors.

We had finished the interiors and were nearly finished the exterior walls when the owner we were working for showed up with policemen. They were there to escort us off his property. We learned later that this property owner had done this very same thing to other builders. The contract he had us sign allowed him to force us off the project for no reason.

By this time, we had invested approximately $250,000 into the project. We hired a lawyer to serve him a summons to appear in court. Unfortunately, this fellow fled the country and the subpoena could not be served. Our credit, which had been very good up to that point, was being destroyed. We owed so much money and no money was coming in to pay the bills.

Unjust Judge

Judge me, O God, and plead my cause against an ungodly nation: O deliver me from the deceitful and unjust man. Psalm 43:1

We waited for a chance to serve our subpoena to the fellow who had cheated us out of our money. We each took odd jobs that came along to make ends meet. Finally, after two years of ruined credit and financial struggle, my brother saw the man who had cheated us and run us off his property. Henry managed to force his way into the house where the man was staying and chased him around a table until finally he was able to touch him with the subpoena. It fell to the floor, but he had been touched by it and we could finally have our day in court. While in session, the judge was so drunk he couldn't even hold his head up for more than a few moments at a time. The judge ruled that we had to pay what had been charged to us and the building owner had to pay what was charged to him. We had already paid $250 000 in expenses, plus there were charge accounts for materials that we had to pay after the court appearance. The charge accounts totalled an additional $150 000. The ruling didn't do us a bit of good and our shifty client got away scot free.

While building the complexes, we hadn't had any authority to charge the purchase of building materials to our client. Our finances had borne all of the charges. We split the debt between the three of us and worked hard to pay it off. I came under the Orderly Payment of Debts program to manage the debt load and worked for years to pay it all off.

The Bride Hunt

And the LORD God said, It is not good that the man should be alone; I will make him an help meet for him. Genesis 2:18

Depressed at what had happened to our family business, I felt as though there was nothing left for me in Calgary. Although my heart had begun to heal, I still missed Myrna and there weren't nearly as many girls to choose from as I would have liked. I was sure that there were more girls in Edmonton so I decided to move there because I wanted to get married and I told my mother my plan.

I made myself a trailer to live in. It was ten feet long and five feet wide. On one side were a door and also a single window. I hooked it up to my little Ford Prefect car, hauled it to Edmonton and parked it at a trailer park. I paid $12 for pad rental each month.

After moving to Edmonton, I started making friends with some of the young people in the area. Donald Schueler, one of my new friends, told me I could park my trailer at his parent's place in the country to save myself from paying rent every month. So I moved it out to their place on 23rd Avenue which is now well within city limits.

I lived in the trailer and worked at Hayward Lumber. I drove my motorcycle back and forth to work. We were building record player cabinets. After that, I started my own shop with my own tools in the Schueler's unused large chicken coop.

Brush with Death

One Monday morning, I was feeling pretty good. Just the previous Friday I had purchased a new Prefect after deciding to retire my old one and I was headed to work. As it was a new car, I was treating it with extra care. For the first 800 miles, we were only supposed to drive the car at a top speed of 30 miles per hour to break in the motor. I had just turned onto the highway and was accelerating slowly.

Suddenly I noticed in my rear view mirror, a car gaining on me rapidly from behind. I swerved into the ditch but the other car smashed into mine from behind. The impact snapped my neck.

When the paramedics arrived, I was rushed to the hospital where the doctors had to put my head back in its proper place. It had been displaced to one side. After the doctors worked on me, they put me in a neck brace that kept my neck bones stationary. The

Chapter 8: New Beginnings

doctors told me it was a miracle that I'd survived the accident much less that I was still able to have the use of my limbs.

When I got out of the hospital, I contacted the drunk driver's insurance company to make a claim on his policy so that I could either fix or replace my wrecked car. I told the agent that due to my broken neck, I was now unable to drive on my motorcycle. The cost of repairing and replacing my car and also my medical expenses had to be covered. The insurance agent told me to sign a form stating what my medical expenses were and the cost of fixing or replacing my vehicle. He told me they would only pay me in one lump sum. I argued that because my medical expenses were still mounting, I could not sign off on the medical expenses but that I needed money for the car right away. I told him I would get a lawyer if he would not give me the money for the car. Then the agent said, "I only work for the company," but there was a form I could sign if I only wanted to get my car fixed. Trusting his word, I signed the form. Not long after that I received a $450 cheque for the car.

After the initial treatments for my neck were completed, I took my bill in to the insurance company to be reimbursed for my expenses, which totalled more than $5 000. The agent laughed at me and told me, "If you are so stupid as to sign the forms without a lawyer, pay for it yourself." I realized then how crooked and deceptive he had been. I always meant to pursue the matter legally but never did get around to it. After all, that was only the cost of the initial expense. Over the years following, I spent many more thousands of dollars in therapy and chiropractic rehabilitation.

After the initial healing in my neck, I began to fix my car. There was an A-frame bar that held the rear axle straight. This bar on one side had collapsed in the accident. Using a blowtorch, I heated the bar and tried to straighten it the best I could. I really should have taken it apart because I never did get it completely straight. I just used a jack and the best pressure I could muster. After that, the rear end always ran a little bit off to the left.

Because it had been all smashed in, the trunk was unusable. So, I built a wooden box that was about a foot deep and stuck out the back about two feet.

Cross-Country Adventure

Later that summer, I was at camp meeting at College Heights and was walking with Donald. I saw a girl about 100 ft away. She caught my attention and I said to Donald, "That's the girl I'm going to marry." I didn't know she was Donald's sister, Shirley.

Donald's mother asked me if I would take her children and Donald's girlfriend on a trip to Banff. She said they wanted to go to the mountains but weren't used to travelling alone and because I was an experienced driver and used to going places on my own, I really must take them. I sensed she had an ulterior motive and, not wanting to be shoved into a relationship with either of her daughters against my will, I said no. However, she was a persistent lady and eventually she wore me down with her pestering.

My friends loaded all the suitcases, tents, and cooking supplies in the box I had built on the back of my car. I even managed to fit my guitar in. Donald, his girlfriend, Esther, his sisters, Shirley and Della, and I all piled into my little car and we were off.

As we drove, the rear axle squealed and howled because, the A-frame bar was twisted and the axle did not line up properly with the gears. I began to doubt whether the car could even make it all the way to Banff and back in its condition. Nevertheless, by the time we arrived in Banff, the howling seemed less noticeable. Perhaps we had gotten used to the sound or it really had gotten better. After spending a couple nights camping in Banff, Esther suggested we drive out to Penticton, British Columbia (BC) where some of her relatives lived.

We all wondered if my car could make it that far. I said I'd be willing to try if they promised not to desert me if the car did break down along the way. Hurriedly, we took down and packed up camp and left that afternoon. We drove into the night on The Big Bend which was a dusty, dirty road. The air inside the car was so dusty that we could literally taste it in our mouths. We took this trip before the highway had been built through Roger's Pass. We stopped and set up camp somewhere near Winfield, BC. The next day we got back on the road and drove the rest of the way to Penticton, close to the US border. We spent time visiting with friends and had a great time.

After a while someone said, "Hey, wouldn't it be cool if we drove into the US?" We all wondered if the car would make it, but because it didn't seem to be any worse for wear, we decided to chance it. We drove to Spokane, Washington (WA) and after visiting Spokane, we decided to visit Oregon (OR). We drove right to the Oregon border and, on the way back, we stopped at Walla Walla, WA overnight.

During the course of our adventure, I began to develop feelings for Shirley. I could tell she had feelings for me, too. But, Della, her older sister, was also attracted to me. It seemed as though Della was always managing to squeeze herself into the car first so that she would be sitting in the middle between Shirley and me.

One afternoon as Shirley and I talked together, I said to her, "Tomorrow, you get into the car before your sister. Then you can sit beside me." So the following day, she was quick to get in the car and we were able to sit beside each other. I could tell that her sister was unhappy about where she was sitting. It took us two days of driving to get back home including the time we took stopping along the way. In those days, we were able to rent a whole log cabin for $10 per night.

The Bride Hunt Comes To an End

After we arrived home, I returned to my job. I began to think about Shirley more and more and we became closer to one another as the days passed by.

Shirley's mother was determined to get us together one way or another. One Friday evening, she had arranged it so that Shirley would be home alone. By this time it was almost as though I was part of the family and I had free access to the house. In fact, I spent more time in the house than I did in my trailer. I went in the house and realized that only Shirley was there. The sun was beginning to set and she was on the couch with her back to me. When she heard me come in, she pointed to the sunset and said, "Oh, Ben, isn't it just beautiful?"

I said, "There is something more beautiful sitting in front of me on the chesterfield." She blushed and then I kissed her for the first time and that was the beginning of our relationship. Not long after that I proposed to Shirley and then we told her parents that we were engaged.

Our New Life Together

When he learned that I was getting married, my good friend Mr. Anderson, offered a small parcel of property where I could build a home for my new bride. So, before we were married, I spent a great deal of time building the house near Mr. Anderson's farm at Stettler. He thought I would manage the farm for him and he would retire. Later he decided to move to BC where his two daughters were living.

Shirley and I were married December 4, 1952. It was one of the happiest days of my life. After the festivities were over, we wearily climbed into our car and drove to Stettler to our new home to spend our first night together as man and wife.

When Mr. Anderson sold his farm the following February, Shirley and I decided to move our house into Stettler. I bought a lot in town and wanted to dig a basement, but the ground was frozen. To thaw it, we spread straw over the ground and then put coal on the straw. We set fire to the straw and the burning straw would light the coal, which smouldered all night. This thawed the ground down approximately one foot during the night. The following day we dug out the thawed ground and repeated the process the next evening until we had dug down deep enough to put in the foundation.

Shirley's brother, Donald, helped me. After we had dug down about two feet we started uncovering metal car parts, old appliances and all other kinds of junk. I had bought the lot from the Town of Stettler, so I went to the office and told them what was happening. The person responsible for selling the lots apologized and said that he had forgotten that that particular lot had been put over an old nuisance ground or garbage dump. He transferred my ownership to another lot a block away and after digging down a couple of feet in the second lot, we ran into the same problem. Again I went back to the town office to complain and again they gave me another lot. And after digging down a few feet, the same problem occurred yet again.

By this time, we had been digging foundations for nearly six weeks. I was so frustrated and I didn't want to go through this process a fourth time. So, we put our footings two feet below the ground and placed approximately three feet of cement blocks above them and then placed the house on top of those. From the outside the house looked like any other house with a basement because I had installed a couple of windows in the cement blocks. I had even made an opening in the back so that the crawl space under the house could be used for storage.

Because the Anderson's had decided to move to British Columbia, Shirley and I didn't really have any reason to stay in the Stettler area anymore. So we advertised the house for sale just as we were doing the finishing work on it. After selling the house we moved to Calgary to be near my parents.

Trucking in Calgary

I started up a cartage business and delivered freight all the way to San Francisco and up the Fairbanks highway and everywhere. Twice one week I went to New Westminster. I had just gotten home from the first trip and someone called who was moving to New Westminster only about two blocks from the last move I had done. Then a big rainstorm came and flooded out the bridges. I called Mom at home and said, "We won't be home for several days. The bridges are flooded out."

After giving our predicament some thought, Dad and I decided we'd fly home and return for the truck when they got the bridges fixed. So that's what we did. Three hours later, we were at the airport near home. We took a taxi home and Mom nearly fell over when she saw us at the door. She wasn't expecting us. "How did you get here?" she said. "I thought you weren't coming."

When the bridges were fixed I went back alone to get the truck. Later that summer, we had to make a trip to Fort St. John. That was such a wet year. Dad came along with me. Beyond Whitecourt, there was no more pavement. It was all gravel road from there. The road was all rutted and people were getting stuck. I had about three tons of furniture on, and having the big wheels on the truck, I went through it all. I got to one place where a bulldozer was working. The operator said, "If you get stuck, I'll just push you through." I said, "No, don't do that. I've just got a wooden box on the back that I built myself. I don't want to smash the good furniture in there."

A Chevy panel van came by. There was a twelve year old girl in the back, just returning from the Mayo Clinic where she had received medical treatment. The car was still under warrantee, but they burned out the clutch trying to get through the mud. I hooked onto them and pulled them a long way, probably around a hundred miles (160 km). Then I left them at a garage.

A little farther along there was a Pontiac in trouble. A rock had gone through the radiator. I hooked onto that car and pulled him along, about fifty miles (80 km) to Fort St. John. When we got there, the bridge was washed out. We had to cross the bridge. We spent a couple of nights in a hotel, waiting to cross the river. The caterpillar was out pushing the mud deeper and deeper to try to get down to hard dirt, making a road to the railway track. The only way across the river was across the train trestle. They didn't even try to fix the road bridge because it had fallen into the river.

I was in a hurry to get back home and I was the first one to go across. A police officer asked me, "Are you sure you can make it across?" I said, "Yes." The trestle was very high and had no sides. I turned the window down on the driver's side and stuck my arm out so I could keep an eye on the rear outside dual wheel, because it was outside the rail. I didn't want to drive it off the ties or we'd have ended up in the river far below. Dad sat right in the middle of the truck, he was so scared.

I put the truck into first gear and went really slowly across the railway ties. Bump, bump, bump. I was partway across when I noticed the bridge waving. I stopped and sure enough, the bridge was waving because I had been going one speed. I thought I'd better go faster and slower to break the rhythm. When I got across to the other side, I told the police, "You'd better tell the people not to go one speed, because that bridge was waving when I went one speed. You've got to go a little faster and a little slower to break the rhythm." He said, "You're a pretty good driver to drive that three ton truck over that narrow railway bridge." It was narrow—just the width of the railway ties. By the grace of God, we made it home safely.

As the business grew more successful, an increasing number of clients wanted to do business with me on Sabbaths. I grew tired of constantly telling people I did not operate on Saturdays. It seemed that clients grew more belligerent each time I told them I would not pick up or deliver their goods on Saturdays. I decided to sell the business.

An Injured Back and Generous Neighbours

Shirley and I moved to Leslieville, near Red Deer, Alberta. We decided to try our hand at farming and bought four quarters. The land we bought, however, was fresh and unbroken, so we knew it would take time and a lot of work before we would make any money from crops. I purchased an old tractor, plough, and a tiller/seeder and began clearing the land.

I made a couple of mistakes when I bought that farm. First, I didn't have crop insurance, because the seller told me, "I've lived here since 1905 and it never hails here. It only hails on the valley, but never up here." Then a fellow came and offered us $125 for the oil rights. I regret not having kept those rights. In 1965, they discovered oil in the area and put five wells on that property.

When I wasn't busy with the farming, I went logging to bring in enough income to make ends meet. The logging kept me so busy, I didn't know how I'd be able to work the land in time to get it seeded. I prayed that God would take care of my situation and then, even though I was unsure of how the Lord would provide, I didn't worry about it anymore.

One day, I crawled under a tree which was propped up on the sawmill landing. As I crawled under it, I bumped it. The tree slipped off and fell on my back, crushing me to the ground. Shirley drove me to the hospital in Edmonton while I lay in the back of the van. The doctors tried all kinds of stretching treatments on me which did not improve the condition of my back. For an entire week we drove back and forth from Shirley's folks' place where we were temporarily staying and the hospital. I worried that we'd lose our farm if I didn't make a quick recovery.

When we returned home, we were shocked to see several tractors, maybe eight to ten, working our land. They worked as a team, breaking, disking, and seeding the land simultaneously. What I could not have hoped to accomplish in more than a month, they completed in two days. I was so thankful to God. The crop was in and it hadn't even cost me any fuel. In fact, one of the farmers had even supplied the seed for the crop. I wanted to pay him but he refused to accept the payment I offered him.

Over the following couple of months, my back gradually healed by itself and I was able to get on with my farming duties.

Our Last Quarter, an Empty Fuel Tank and Miracle Money

Fall arrived and harvest time was fast approaching. One Friday I said to Shirley, "We owe for several pails of fuel at the service station. We can't afford to pay what we owe. In fact, we don't have any money; we are literally down to our last quarter." Our fuel tank was nearly empty and we wanted to attend church the next day but there wasn't enough fuel in the car to get us to the nearest church at College Heights. Shirley and I knelt and prayed about our situation. I knew that God would have a way for us to get to church. After our prayer, I felt impressed to go into Leslieville to pick up the mail.

Among the mail was a cheque for $52.00. A letter explained that the Workers Compensation Board had overcharged me three years earlier. Thanking the Lord for His many blessings, I rejoiced all the way to the service station, where I filled up the car with fuel, and I continued rejoicing as I drove home.

The following morning we got ready for church. We stepped out the front door and were greeted by golden stalks of wheat waving to us in the gentle breeze. I felt as though God couldn't be nearer to us than at that very moment. Despite my previous injury, God had impressed others to cultivate and plant the land for me so that my crop would get in on time. The tasks had actually been completed sooner than they would have been if I hadn't been injured and had completed the work on my own.

Now it was fall and the crop was nearly ready to harvest. The stalks had turned a beautiful golden yellow. They were tall and the grains were so full they appeared as though they'd burst if they were any fuller. The fields really were a lovely sight to behold. As if all that weren't enough to assure us of how much God loved us, He had provided a goodly sum of money at just the very moment when we needed it the very most. I felt so high that it was all I could do to keep myself from shouting for joy.

That morning, we drove to church with a real sense of peace. We enjoyed a lovely service and were invited to share lunch with the Schafer's in their home. Toward evening, we returned home. As we passed the fields, I looked over at them. The stalks were no longer waving playfully in the breeze. The entire crop looked like a summer fallowed field.

Hailed Out

I walked the fields. There wasn't a single stalk of wheat left standing. Hail had destroyed everything while we were at church. The scene before me was surreal and I just couldn't seem to understand why God had let it happen.

I knew that when it came time for me to make the farm payment to the farmer I'd bought the land from that I wouldn't have any money. Due to money I owed on the apartment building fiasco in Calgary, my credit was in shambles. I knew I would not be able to borrow money from the bank, so, I advertised the land for sale. Within two to three weeks I had lined up a buyer for one quarter. He agreed to take over my contract on it and gave me $1100.00 and a brand new car as a down payment. The payment that was due was

$750.00, so I paid that and had $350.00 left over and the car. The person I sold the farm to wanted to move in the following spring so we were able to stay on the farm for several months after that.

Chapter 9: Hardship and Angel Choirs

Nothing to Do and Nowhere to Go

When it came time for us to move, we loaded our possessions into a trailer hitched to our Studebaker and climbed into the car without knowing what we would do or where we were going.

Before driving away, we bowed our heads in prayer and asked the Lord to show us where he wanted us to go. I suggested we go to Calgary as my family was down there. She suggested we go to Edmonton as her family was up there. After we had driven for a while, we still hadn't decided where we should go, so we pulled over to the side of the road and prayed again that the Lord would lead us to the right place.

The thought to go to Balten[1] entered our minds but we quickly dismissed it because there were only eight people attending the Seventh-day Adventist Church there. We knew that the members were hostile and unkind to one another and that the church was about to close its doors for good because the members were unable to solve their differences. After living so far away from an Adventist church, it was important to us that we live nearby to one.

We drove for a while more and by this time we were travelling north and still as undecided as ever. Once again, we pulled to the side of the road to pray. We continued our drive this way throughout the day. In fact, if I recall correctly, as we made our way we pulled to the side of the road to pray for guidance at least five or six different times. By evening we found ourselves driving down the main street of Balten. It was one of those blink-and-you-miss-it towns. Main Street was where all the appeal and attraction was supposed to be but there was neither appeal nor attraction in my heart for this little town. Secretly, I hoped that this wasn't where God intended us to stay.

How Could This Be God's Place for Us?

I stopped the car, rested my hands on the steering wheel and voiced my thoughts out loud, "Lord, why on earth did you lead us to this God-forsaken town?" Only moments later, a stranger walked over to us and said, "Are you looking for a place to rent?" I told him, "We don't know what we're doing or where we're supposed to be and haven't made up our minds yet." He responded by saying, "Maybe I could help you make up your mind. My house is empty. If you'd like, you could move right in. It's just right across the road."

---

1 Name has been changed

I told him that we didn't have any money to pay for rent. "That's alright," he said, "I can tell you're trustworthy. You can pay as you're able. Honestly, I really wouldn't mind if you moved in right now."

I looked at Shirley and she was looking at me. I could tell that she was also thinking that this was God's way of answering our prayers. Otherwise, there seemed no logical explanation as to why a perfect stranger had approached us from across the street and offered to let us move into his house immediately, all without any money up front and not even a promise of when the funds would materialize.

I told him that we'd like to see the house before we made our final decision and he brought us to see it. It was a little, one bedroom house but we were only a family of three (our daughter Marlene was six years old at the time) and didn't need a lot of space. After seeing the house, my mind became peaceful and I rested knowing that the Lord must surely have planned for us to be here.

Buying Without Money

After settling in, I began to wonder what I could do for work. I went looking and discovered the Auction Mart. The Auction Mart had been used for cattle sales but had recently closed due to bankruptcy. The building was vacant and not being used. I approached the owner about renting the building. He said that would be okay as he wasn't using it for anything. I started selling odd equipment and repairing televisions out of it. As a result, I was able to rekindle the Auction Mart and hold auctions once per week but I was unable to get the rights to sell cattle due to its previous bankruptcy.

After a while, I bought an old CAT[2] and began using it to work up farmers' fields and clear their land. I kept myself pretty busy with the auctions on Sundays, doing CAT work during the weekdays, and repairing televisions, tractors, odd equipment and pretty much anything else anyone brought to me in the evenings.

Hostility and Hurt, Healing and Restoration

If a man say, I love God, and hateth his brother, he is a liar: for he that loveth not his brother whom he hath seen, how can he love God whom he hath not seen? 1 John 4:20

There were only eight people attending the Balten Seventh-day Adventist Church when we moved there. After attending the church for a number of weeks we became aware of the turmoil within the church. Of utmost concern to us was the open hostility—hatefulness, spitefulness, and even physical violence—displayed by the members towards one another. We made it our mission to help the members repair their damaged relationships.

Each week we invited a bunch of people to our home for lunch, including two families that were at odds with one another. After a few weeks, we had had all the hostile families to our house for lunch save two. I knew these families were bitter enemies. Things were so

---

2   Short form for Caterpillar—a manufacturer of construction and mining equipment and a wide range of other equipment.

bad between them that if one family attended church, the other family would not.

In our home, the kitchen and living room were divided by a partition. One particular day, all of the families we had invited had already arrived but one. Everyone chatted in the living room as they waited for lunch to begin -- everyone that is but I. I waited and watched from the kitchen window for the other family to arrive. I saw their family car pull up and then when the driver spotted the other family's car, he began to turn around. Quickly I hurried from the house and, as though I didn't realize what he was doing, invited him in. Not wanting to admit they didn't want to come in because of the other family, they protested and said, "But you have so many people over already. Surely you don't have enough room or food for us." There were probably forty or forty-five people at our house which was quite a bit more than had been at church. I told him there was plenty of room and food and that after we ate lunch we were going to be singing songs. "Come in and enjoy yourselves," I insisted. They reluctantly agreed and came in.

After that they were all at our home for the following few Saturday nights. One night I said something that I'm certain only the Lord could have impressed me to say. Although I don't remember exactly what I said, I spoke about how if we couldn't learn to love one another, we would never make it to heaven. The families that had been fighting amongst themselves began weeping. They hugged, asked for forgiveness, and received forgiveness from each other. After that we all sang, "Praise God, from Whom All Blessings Flow." Soon afterward, we began making plans to build a new church.

Past Debts

Take, my brethren, the prophets, who have spoken in the name of the Lord, for an example of suffering affliction, and of patience. Behold, we count them happy which endure. James 5: 10, 11

After about five years in Balten, our "old life" caught up with our "new life," so to speak. Bills from the apartment building fiasco still haunted us. We just couldn't keep up with all of the demands. Every time we turned around something was getting seized. First our car was confiscated and then the CAT I depended on so heavily for the bulk of our income. The companies kept removing anything of value from our possession to pay down our debts. An elder of the church told me that my personal debt was making the church look bad. That was an additional blow. I had enough heartache already. But heartaches only make us stronger if we trust God.

To top it all off, Shirley was not well. She blacked out and we rushed to her Edmonton hospital. She had had an aneurism. A few months later it happened again. They did two brain surgeries on her within months of each other.

Heart Attack

About two weeks after Shirley's second operation while she rested in the house, I was

Chapter 9: Hardship and Angel Choirs

putting plaster board on the porch. Suddenly I noticed a strange feeling in my chest. My heart was doing something odd. An elderly man was visiting with me and he saw that I was in pain and about to pass out. He grabbed me and picked me up and called someone from help. A couple of neighbours heard him cry out and came over to help. That's all I remember.

The next thing I knew, I heard someone say, "We're going 90 miles an hour." They were driving me to the hospital.

I woke up in intensive care and was there recovering for ten days. I wondered why Shirley hadn't come to see me. I learned later that Shirley had a third aneurism a day after I had the heart attack.

During my stay in hospital, someone from the church visited me and brought me the *Desire of Ages*. I had nothing else to do, so I sceptically started reading it. I was not a fan of Ellen White's at the time. Someone had told me she was a false prophet, so I avoided her books. In the hospital, I flipped through the first part of the book and thought, "Ellen White's junk." I skipped around in the book a bit. Every time I stopped to read a section, though, I was struck by Mrs. White's passionate retelling of the events of Jesus' life. It was like she was an eye witness. And when I read the part about Jesus dying on the cross, I felt like I was there myself, that He saw me and died for me personally. I was never the same after reading that book.

During the time I was in the hospital, Shirley had her third brain surgery, but the doctors couldn't do anything for her. The aneurism was too deep. We were discharged from the hospital at the same time. Before we left, Shirley's doctor met with me privately and told me she had only three months to live. Shirley complained that she was hearing a noise in her head. She said, "It sounds like water going back and forth—swish, swish, swish, swish."

I was so discouraged. Shirley was dying. I had no money to pay Shirley's medical bills and Marlene's tuition. I hadn't been paid for the last three jobs I had done for farmers. I prayed about it and God sent Mr. Clark who told me someone was paying Marlene's tuition for school. That was one problem solved. At least Marlene would be able to continue her schooling. I should have been thankful, but I was anxious instead. My money problems were crushing me.

The Day I Left God

When I went back to work at the Auction Mart, I bought four big heavy army generators. The guy who sold them to me told me they were brand new and had never been used. He said they'd be good for welders. I put a car engine on one and spun it and I couldn't get it to work. No way. And here I'd bought four of them. They cost me $500 a piece.

It seemed like the only way people got ahead was to lie. I got thinking, It seems all the wicked guys are making money and I'm going broke. It seemed so unfair. I resented being tricked into buying generators that didn't work and I was desperate to get my money out of them.

I loaded one onto my truck and made a deal with a fellow who traded a car for the generator. I was in a hurry to get out of there because I didn't want him to try and start it up and find out that it didn't work. Then I'd have been on the spot.

Loaded with guilt and grief over Shirley, I thought I'd go see Henry with the car. The fellow who traded it to me told me it needed some work and I knew Henry could help me with it. When I got near Beiseker, I started to cry. I said, "God where are you?" I turned off the road and drove toward the Rosebud Church east of Beiseker. I parked the truck on the highway about a mile and a half from the church and just sat there. I could see the church off in the distance in the moonlight. It was a beautiful night, but I felt so ugly inside. I lay my head back and just cried. My heart hurt so badly, I thought it would just stop. I said to God, "I've been going to church all my life. I gave my life to you and my wife is dying and I'm broke. I'm not getting paid for the work that I do. What's the use?" I felt like giving up.

Angels' Voices

Suddenly, I heard the most beautiful singing I'd ever heard in my life. The singing was loud, like they were singing inside the cab of the truck. In quartet style the voices sang a song written by Henry F. Lyte:

Jesus I my cross have taken,
All to leave and follow thee;
All things else have I forsaken,
Thou from hence my all shall be.

The angels sang beautifully. Earthly music is horrible in comparison. God was reminding me of His love for me. It changed my thinking. I asked God to forgive me for my faithless words and behaviour. What a loving God we have. I had hope again.

I went on to Calgary and got to my parents' home at 4:30 in the morning. I went in and sat down at the organ and played this song. Everybody was crying. I went back home feeling better.

Once home, I got back to tinkering with the generators. I noticed an arrow on the housing I hadn't seen before. The arrow pointed in the opposite direction of the direction I had been spinning the starter. When I spun it counter-clockwise, it started. The generators I'd bought actually did work. They welded perfectly. I had just done something wrong. So the one I'd sold the guy did work after all. I was so relieved.

Miracle of Healing

About this time, I wrote to the Voice of Prophecy and the Quiet Hour, both Adventist radio programs. They take prayer requests. I didn't tell my wife that the doctor had said she only had three months to live. I just couldn't tell her. Besides, I knew God could heal her if He wanted to. One night, I stayed out in the garage a long time and just prayed. I

Chapter 9: Hardship and Angel Choirs

went in at 9 p.m.

"Ben," Shirley said, "that noise quit."

I said, "I've been praying and the Voice of Prophecy and the Quiet Hour were praying at 8 o'clock this morning." God heard our prayers and healed her. After that, Shirley was well enough to work and had a job for eight years at the College Heights book bindery.

Buying without Money

I told Shirley, "We really need another CAT. A lot of people have bush they want me to clear for them and I just can't do it without a machine. Besides, I can't make payments on our debts if I can't work." We prayed about it and Shirley said, "How will you be able to get one without money?"

Claiming one of God's promises and quoting from the Bible, I told her, "The Lord says, come and buy without money and without price.[3] I'll just go up to Edmonton and see what I can find," I said. "What's the use of going all that way and wasting all that fuel, if nothing will come of it," Shirley countered. "I just think I should go," I responded.

So, that day, I drove up to Edmonton praying the whole way. I stopped at a business called Lahore Machinery (if I recall correctly) which was owned by Paul Lahore. The salesperson who worked with me was Jason and up front I told him my situation. "I have work lined up," I said then proceeded cautiously, "but no money and no credit."

He replied, "You look like a man I can trust. There are two D9-G CATs that just came in last night. The starting engine on one of them isn't working." That was the biggest CAT they made at the time. It weighed 45 tons. God knew what I needed before I even got there.

Encouraged, I eagerly said, "I could fix the starting engine. I'll take that one if it's okay but I need to confirm that you understand I have no money."

"I believe I can trust you," he replied again. "Come into the office and we can fill out the paperwork." We went into the office and I continued to pray that this deal would not fail. I needed the machine to do the work I had lined up and to pay our mounting bills. He drew up the contract and it stated that I could pay for the CAT as I was able. When I made money, I would pay them and if I wasn't working, I wasn't required to pay until I had money again. After he had been so kind to draw up the paperwork and be sensitive of my financial needs, I said, "This is all so wonderful, but I still see one problem."

"What's that?" he asked.

"I don't even have enough money to pay to have it delivered to where I live. I imagine it would be pretty expensive to have a big machine like that hauled."

"I can solve that problem for you," he said and phoned Miller Trucking while I sat in the office with him. He told them he needed them to make a delivery for him and to charge it to the dealership.

I followed the truck home and they delivered it right into my yard. Shirley couldn't believe her eyes when she saw the machine. The Lord was really good to me. That was

---

[3] Isaiah 55:1

one of the best things that ever happened to me. In a day and a half I had fixed the engine. After that, Miller trucking agreed to move the CAT to my next jobsite and let me pay them when I had finished the job. Every time I needed it moved, they moved it for me. That machine never let me down. Many times it was put to the test and always worked faithfully. Shirley and I were able to pay off our debts with the money we made clearing land for others.

Several years later, it was still running well and I no longer needed it. A gentleman in Lacombe offered to buy it from me and I sold it to him. What a blessing that CAT was.

College Heights

A little while later, the Lord moved us out of Balten. We loaded all our household things onto a trailer along with the CAT and drove to College Heights where Marlene was enrolled in college. I had lived in a shack just off campus and I thought maybe we'd find a house available for rent. There was an old house that hadn't been lived in for four or five years. We parked everything in front of the house and wondered what to do next.

Just then the owners of the house drove up. That very day, the owners of the house had left their home in Salmon Arm, BC and headed for their College Heights property. They told me they had an overwhelming urge to come to the house, though they had no reason to. They stopped several times enroute, trying to decide whether to continue on or not. They prayed about it, but the urge to continue driving till they got there just wouldn't leave.

When they arrived and saw me standing in front of their house, the woman said to her husband, "Oh look. It's Benny." It was the same couple I'd rented the little shack from when I went to school.

She said to me, "What are you doing here?"

I said, "Well, truthfully, I'm looking for a place to rent. My daughter is going to school here now and we'd like to get a place near campus so we can be with her."

They said, "Well the house is empty. You can move in right now. It's for sale."

I said, "What do you want for it?"

"We're asking $4 500."

I had just gotten a cheque for $2 800 and was going to cash it the next day. It was all the money I had and I knew that it wasn't enough, but I made the offer anyway.

She said, "We'll talk it over." They walked a little distance away and talked. When they came back they said, "You can have it for $2 800. You settle in for the night and we'll come back in the morning to close the deal."

I thought, This is a bargain. So we started moving the stuff in. The neighbour came and helped us. We would get to sleep in our own house that very night. How we counted our blessings!

Just before we crawled into bed, the couple returned. I thought, Oh, no. They're backing out of the deal. I'm sure they want more.

They said, "Ben we've been thinking. You did so much for us. You took us to church and you took us to Calgary and you fixed our car. We never gave you anything for all the things you did." Then they added, "There's another lot adjoining this one—it's a big one—we're going to throw in that lot, too."

What a blessing! The Lord is so generous. I could never out-give the Lord, but I want to be like Him. I may not have remembered doing anything for these people, but God brought to their memory something I'd done for them years back and whenever we give to others, He promises to bless us in ways we can't even imagine. A favourite Scripture of mine says, *Give, and it shall be given unto you; good measure, pressed down, and shaken together, and running over, shall men give into your bosom. For with the same measure that ye mete withal it shall be measured to you again. Luke 6:38*

All Things are Possible

With God all things are possible. Matthew 19: 26

I had to work so I knew that somehow, I was going to have to replace the machinery that I'd lost before moving to College Heights. I told my wife I was going to Calgary to get a used rototiller somewhere.

I got to the rototiller company, but they didn't have any used ones on hand and the new ones were too much. The salesman said, "I know where there's one. It's at Bragg Creek. You should look at it. It's only got thirteen hours on it."

I said, "No, that would be a lot of money. I was expecting to get something for three or four thousand and finance it, yet."

But he talked me into going out with him to look at the equipment. The salesman introduced me to Wilbur and we looked at the equipment together. It was almost brand new. I asked Wilbur what he wanted for it.

"Twenty-five thousand," he said.

I said, "I told the salesman not to bring me out here because I'm trying to find something that I can finance. I was actually hoping to find someone who might be kind enough to finance one for me."

Wilbur said, "Well, you look like a fellow I could trust. We'll just sign an empty slip and you pay as you can."

I couldn't believe it. I returned with the salesman to the dealership, got my car, a Ford Galaxy, and went back to the farmer's place.

"How are you going to get the equipment home?" he asked me.

I had welded an angle iron onto the bumper of the car—in those days, bumpers were strong. I said, "I'm going to pull it home."

"It's 12 tons!" he exclaimed.

I said, "Well I've done dumber things before. I'll just go slow." Wilbur was scratching his head, but he helped me hook it up. Wilbur's son came out with a movie camera and took my picture as I left.

I came down to Richmond Road. It was spring time and the road crew had scattered pea gravel on the ice. I tried to stop when the light turned red, but I couldn't slow down. The heavy machine was pushing the car this way and that way. I had to take my foot off the brake so the car would straighten out. I was coming up to the intersection and the car was sliding slowly, but it wasn't stopping.

A trucker saw me struggling to get the car under control. He was driving a big truck with a high-boy trailer. He turned his truck sideways and blocked the road to let me get safely through. After that I began braking a long way from intersections to be sure I was pretty near stopping before I got to an intersection. I pulled the rototiller all the way home without incident.

Then I told Shirley, "Now I need a big four wheel drive tractor." Maybe she thought I was crazy, but she didn't say so. She knew I didn't have the money to buy a big tractor, but I trusted the Lord to provide me with the equipment I needed to earn my living.

I went to a tractor dealer in Red Deer and told him I needed a tractor to pull the rototiller I'd just bought.

"It doesn't have to be that good," I told him. "Something that's cheap would work for me. I have a bit of a problem. My finances are bad. I was looking at that old tractor there," I said pointing at a relic that had seen better days. I didn't even know if the thing ran, but I figured I could probably make a deal with the guy on it. I figured I could probably fix it up and use it till I'd made enough money to get a better one.

The dealer said, "You have a new rototiller, you should have a new tractor."

I said, "Oh, that's an expense I just can't afford right now."

"No," he said, "Come on over here. We just got three in." He pointed out a shining new red Massey Harris 1805 with dual wheels and said, "That's the best tractor. You take that one."

"I explained to you," I said patiently, "I don't have any finances."

"Don't worry about that," he said. "You take it. We'll work the finances out later."

So I drove away with my car hooked up behind the tractor.

Chapter 10: Working for God, Rototilling to Pay the Bills

Rototilling Business

I hired a man to do brush piling, pushing bush down and laying them in windrows with a CAT, west of Ponoka. I often talked to him about God. One day he came to me and said, "Look at my fingers." I couldn't see anything wrong with them and I wondered if he'd gotten hurt.

He said, "Haven't you noticed? I haven't smoked in six weeks and you didn't even notice!" When he was smoking, his fingers had been yellow.

"Oh!" I said. "I'm sorry for not noticing."

"Well, Ben I just wanted you to know that you inspired me and I want to get baptized."

That's how my life started out in Lacombe. Thank God for moving us out of Balten, because it just seemed that everything was going my way in Lacombe. I loved witnessing for Jesus and it seemed that He often sent people to me who were searching for Him.

Then I started rototilling. At my first job in the area, I told the farmer God loves him. The farmer attended the Christian Reform Church, but he was searching for the truth. After that, we had talks about the Bible. I told the pastor of our local church about the farmer and he went out and gave him Bible studies and the farmer got baptized. I thanked God for that. That was a start to my missionary work.

That first farmer sent me to a friend's farm and I rototilled there. I went from one Christian Reform farm to another. I think I rototilled all the farms around there. I was really blessed.

I was doing well financially during that time, also. I made $82 000 that summer on Christian Reform farms.

One day I was working for one of the Christian Reform church members in that area and another member of that congregation came to me and said, "Don't work for this guy, Ben. He's one of the bad sheep. He doesn't pay his bills."

I felt bad about that. I'd already started and wanted to finish the work. I went ahead and worked anyway. I said, "I'll take a chance on it." That fellow came back and checked on my progress every day. Then a bunch of them got together and one handed me a cheque for the work I'd completed. The church members backed up the wayward member and paid his bill for him.

I found that the Christian Reform farmers I met liked talking about the Bible. I sat with one of them one night out against the tractor under the moonlight talking about the Bible till two in the morning. My wife wondered what happened, because it was Sabbath and I always came home early on Fridays. But the farmer had come out at 4 p.m. just as I was getting ready to go home and we got talking. We talked till late.

One of them that used to come and see me would drive into the yard and put his head on the steering wheel and just cry. He knew he should keep the Sabbath. I'd go over and reach my hand through the window and put my hand on his shoulder. He said, "You know, you're right about what you teach on the Sabbath. I want to do what's right, but my wife…"

I said, "I know. That's going to hurt."

"She's the organist for the Christian Reform Church and she doesn't want anything to do with the Adventists. It's making it bad for us."

I said, "Well, the Lord says you've got to be willing to leave father and mother, sister, brother, husband or wife. But you pray to God about it and you make the right move." He came back twice like that, crying. He stopped the truck and laid his head on the steering wheel and just cried. I've seen him off and on over the years and we are good friends but he hasn't made the stand yet.

Door to Door

And as ye go, preach, saying, The kingdom of heaven is at hand. Matthew 10: 7

When I went from house-to-house soliciting funds for charitable organizations such as ADRA,[1] I was always frightened, even if I went with someone. In addition, just the thought of taking literature, particularly Adventist literature, to Sunday keeping people sent chills up and down my spine. I literally hated doing it.

Nevertheless, my heart was burning with desire to let others know about the Jesus I had met. I felt that if I did not tell others, my own spiritual fervour would wane and eventually die. I knew it wasn't right to keep what I had learned about Jesus to myself and while I drove the rototiller I prayed that God would use me to help people.

I remembered someone giving me the book *The Desire of Ages* when I was in the Edmonton University Hospital recovering from my heart attack. That book made such an impression on me that my whole life changed after reading it. I started thinking that maybe I should distribute door to door *The Desire of Ages* and other books like it. I drove to the Alberta Conference Office and purchased two boxes of books each containing 40 copies of *The Desire of Ages*. In addition, I already had in my possession 400 copies of a little pamphlet circulated by The Quiet Hour Ministries[2] titled *When Days Are Dark*.

---

1   The Adventist Development and Relief Agency
2   Pastor J. L. Tucker founded Quiet Hour Ministries as a radio program in 1937. Under God's miraculous leading, inspiration, and blessing, the ministry has blossomed into worldwide evangelism and high-tech global communications.

Chapter 10: Working for God, Rototilling to Pay the Bills

How God Cured My Fear of Going Door-to-Door

There is no fear in love; but perfect love casteth out fear: because fear hath torment. He that feareth is not made perfect in love. 1 John 4:18

One Sabbath I worked up enough nerve to go from house to house and give them away. I got into my truck and drove south out of town, then headed west on Morningside Road. I approached the first farm and slowed to turn into the drive, but I lost my nerve and continued driving slowly on down the road. I even drove past the next farm. My jangly nerves were paralyzing me from accomplishing my goal. After that I came to an intersection and turned north. I knew I just had to get over myself and start going up to the houses or my fear would overtake me.

I made my mind up to go to the next home and made myself turn in to the drive. The house was close to the road and as I turned in, I saw a man standing by the garage. I was already so nervous that the sight of him made me downright fearful. Quickly, I decided to make like I was just turning around and as I did that I opened my door and "accidentally" tossed out a copy of *When Days Are Dark*.

I went back south, and because my nerves were bothering me so much, I pulled into a clearing in the trees alongside the road which was about a mile and a half down from where I'd just been and parked. Mentally exhausted, I laid my head on the back of the truck seat and said, "God, I can't do this!" For the longest time I just stayed there wondering what I was going to tell Shirley. How was I going to explain to her that I had gotten all these books only to be too afraid to give them out? I prayed and wept and kept telling God that I just wasn't cut out to do this. I'm not sure how long I was there but it must have been at least an hour and a half. Eventually, I had to go home.

I reoriented my vehicle and headed back the same direction from which I'd earlier come. Nervously I approached the drive where I had tossed out the pamphlet only to see that the man who had been standing by his garage was now sitting on the ground at the end of his driveway, reading the very book I had dropped. When he saw me, he motioned me to come up to him. Well, I couldn't very well refuse to drive up there. Shaking nervously, I turned in and wondered what he would have to say to me. I was always scared of reprisals.

I stopped the truck and got out. The man pointed to the pamphlet I had dropped and said, "You dropped this by accident. It's a lovely little book. Have you got any other literature?"

"Yes," I said with great relief. "As a matter of fact I happen to have another book called *The Desire of Ages*." I handed one to him and after that we talked for quite a while about the Bible.

The incident got my courage up and after I left there, I went to the other two farms that I had missed earlier and left literature at each one. After that I continued passing out literature all over the place for several more years. I haven't kept perfect track of everything I've handed out but I believe I've passed out well over 3 000 copies of *The Desire of Ages* alone. I can safely say, I've passed out 10 000 books. Over the years I also periodically passed out pamphlets and several other books. This has served to be a tremendous blessing in my life.

"Everyone Seems to Think You Belong in Their Home"

One Sabbath, Don Corkum, the pastor of the College Heights Seventh-day Adventist Church, invited Shirley and me to lunch. He told me that he had heard I was going door-to-door handing out books and then told me that he was encouraging his members to do the same thing but that everyone was too timid to do it. He asked if he could go along with me. I readily agreed and even told him that I wished he would take over for me.

"No, no," he said, "I want to see how you do it."

When I got to the houses I'd have the book in my hands and I'd ring the doorbell or knock on the door. When someone came to the door I'd say something like, "I have a book to give you that has changed my whole life. When I was in the hospital I read it through and it just made my whole life different. I really feel like everyone should have the chance to have such a life changing book so that's why I'm here to give you one." Most times I would be invited in. We would talk awhile and sometimes we'd even have prayer together.

When Pastor Corkum came with me that afternoon, we went to Stettler, over 50 miles (80 km) away. I followed the same routine and we went from house to house until sundown. We didn't even stop for supper. Although we hadn't eaten dinner, we didn't feel hungry. The sun was setting as we drove home and we both sensed the peace of heaven. It was such an inexplicable feeling, but our hearts overflowed with joy. We conversed as we drove and Pastor Corkum noted with incredulity, "Everyone seems to think you belong in their home." By the time we finally reached his house it was nearly 11:00 p.m.

Respect Begets Respect

No matter who I rototilled for, I was always able to talk about the Bible with every farmer I worked for. A colony of Mennonites living near Big Valley asked me to do some rototilling for them. I worked a few days and then it was Friday. No matter where I was working I always quit early on Friday to guard the beginning edge of the Sabbath at sundown.

After seeing that I was wrapping things up, the head elder of the colony walked out to me and asked, "I suppose you'll be wanting to come out and work on Sunday?"

"No," I said. "I know that you folks worship on Sunday and I don't want to dishonour your day of worship."

After that he wanted to know why I worshipped on Saturday. I told him I kept Saturday holy because it was the Sabbath of the Bible. I read the commandments to him and he read along silently.

Remember the sabbath day, to keep it holy.
Six days shalt thou labour, and do all thy work:
But the seventh day is the sabbath of the LORD thy God: in it thou shalt not do any work, thou, nor thy son, nor thy daughter, thy manservant, nor thy maidser-

Chapter 10: Working for God, Rototilling to Pay the Bills

vant, nor thy cattle, nor thy stranger that is within thy gates:

For in six days the LORD made heaven and earth, the sea, and all that in them is, and rested the seventh day: wherefore the LORD blessed the sabbath day, and hallowed it.
Exodus 20: 8-11

I got ready to leave and was about to say, "I'll see you Monday," when he said to me, "The Bible says 'six days shalt thou labour' and if I keep you from coming on Sunday, I'd be imposing on your religion, so you just come and till on Sunday. I really want you to because I'll feel guilty if you don't."

I told him I wouldn't feel right coming and working in the fields during their day of worship. However, he insisted that he wanted me to come. "I'm concerned about what the Bible says", he noted. Despite his insistence, I told him I would not be there on Sunday. I also told him that he needn't worry about my not working six days per week because I had plenty of chores at home that could be done on Sundays. I often repaired and maintained rototiller parts on Sundays so that my machines wouldn't break down during the week.

A Broken Marriage and Buried Bed Springs

After finishing my work at Big Valley, I went to Ferrintosh to rototill for a fellow named Dennis who lived next to a colony of Mennonites. After I'd been rototilling for two or three days, the head elder of the colony came and introduced himself. The elder of the local Mennonite church came asked me to come and talk to a couple who hadn't been to church in the last four or five years. The elder told me that they had been faithful, long-time church members, but something had gone wrong. They had quit coming to church and were sleeping in separate beds.

I said, "I can't do anything, but the Holy Spirit can."

Not long after talking with that Mennonite elder, I was contracted to do some work for a farmer who lived across the road from the couple the elder had talked to me about. I took my rototiller to the field and wondered how I would approach the couple who lived in the house across the road. I didn't know the people. I couldn't walk up to the door and start talking to a couple of strangers about their marriage.

"Lord, how do I start?" I asked. "What do I say?" But there were no answers.

I got to work on the farmer's field. I was there to do custom farm work, but I was troubled about the couple across the road. The Lord had not opened the way and I could not think of any way to approach them.

I'd completed a few rounds on the field and as I made another pass, the couple's house came into view once more. I was surprised to see a man walking from the house out onto the field to meet me. I shut off the machinery so I could talk with him.

"I've got a mess of brush on about an acre of land in front of the house, there," the man said, pointing his thumb over his shoulder toward the house behind him. "I was wondering if you could come over and till that up for me."

I told the man that I would come right over. He was happy with that and turned and I followed him with the machinery across the road to the little field in front of the house. Now I'll have a chance to talk with him, I thought to myself. As I worked his field, I prayed for the right words to say. "How do I start?" I asked the Lord again. But there was no answer and I came up blank. Even as the man came up to the tractor to thank me and pay for the work I'd done, I could think of no way to talk with him about his marriage problems.

"Lord, I blew it," I prayed as the man went back into his house. I didn't want to let the Mennonite elder down. I didn't want to leave the place without having said a word of encouragement to the man about his troubled marriage. And most of all, I didn't want to let God down, because I felt that I was there to do more than just rototill a farmer's field. But, I was at a complete loss as to how I could help this couple.

With a heavy heart, I returned to the field across the road and continued with the rototilling. I hadn't done more than a couple of rounds when I saw the man leaving his house and crossing the road once again to come and meet me.

"That acre of ground that you tilled looks so nice now," he began, "Could you come and do the yard around the house?"

Well, there's one thing I hate doing, and that's rototilling a yard. I know some guys who do custom rototilling who flat out refuse to work people's yards because you never know what kind of junk you're going to churn up—anything from utility wires to tangled fencing. The down time that results from breaking machinery on stuff buried in the yard just isn't worth it.

I felt that the Lord was giving me another opportunity to help this man though, so I said, "Yes! I'll be right over."

The man showed me the three acres of land nearest to the house that he wanted tilled up and I went to work, praying all the while that God would show me a way to reach this man for Him.

I had been tilling only a few minutes when suddenly, there was a terrible racket. Sure enough, I'd hit something. The man came hurrying out of the house to see what had made the awful noise. I jumped down from the tractor and went around to the back of the equipment. A rusty old bed spring stuck out of the freshly tilled soil. Part of it was mixed up in the equipment.

The man offered to help and we went down on our knees under the machine to untangle the mess. As we worked on the mangled bits of metal, I said, "That's the way some people's lives are, all messed up like that."

The fellow stopped yanking at the metal for a moment and looked at me. "Well, Ben," he said slowly. "That's how my life is."

"I'm sorry to hear that," I told him. "What's the trouble?"

"My wife and I aren't getting along," he said. "We haven't been for a long time."

"Have you prayed about it?" I asked.

"No," he said shaking his head sadly.

Chapter 10: Working for God, Rototilling to Pay the Bills

"Let's pray right now," I said and I put my arm around his shoulder and prayed with him, kneeling there in the dirt under the equipment.

When I finished praying, I told him, "Go and pray with your wife. You can't wait for her to apologize."

The fellow nodded his head and told me he would. He crawled out from under the machinery and went into the house. I finally freed the equipment from the bed spring and went back to tilling the yard.

It took about three hours to complete the work. I didn't see the man the whole time and I wondered how things were going. I prayed a lot for that couple as I worked in their yard.

When the work was done, the man came out with his wife and they were holding hands. As the couple approached, I could see that the wife had been crying, but she looked happy. She thanked me sincerely and I went back to the field across the road.

When I went to leave, she even kissed me on the cheek. I thank God that He was able to use me that day to help that man.

Free Fuel

While doing a job, I would leave the rototiller on location until the job was finished. I would drive out each morning with my truck and empty the fuel tank in the back of my truck to fill up the rototiller's and the tractor's tanks. Full tanks were generally enough to last all day.

The next Monday, I was still marvelling at how the Lord had intervened and used me to reach this man and his wife. I had just filled the tractor tank and started working the field when I saw the church elder drive up to my truck, get into it, and drive it away. I wasn't really concerned. After all, he'd left his truck behind. I was just puzzled as to why he'd done that. I was on the far side of the field or else I'd have gone over to find out what he was doing. A little while later, he returned with my truck. I drove up and asked what was going on.

"Ben," he said, "I just wanted to do something nice for you."

Because I had filled up the tiller that morning before I started working, the 250 gallon tank on the back of my truck was empty. He had taken my truck back to his place and filled up the large tank and filled up my truck, as well.

I asked, "What did you do that for?"

"You should have been at church yesterday," he replied. "Geoff and his wife were sitting close to each other holding hands. Everyone was really happy. It was the happiest day I can remember in our church." Before I left for home that day, I thanked God for the blessing and I thanked Him again for working through me to help Geoff and his family.

Only a few days later I was doing another tilling job in Ferrintosh for Eldon and Harold, two young Pentecostal brothers when their brother Ron, the head elder of the Pentecostal Church drove up. He got into my truck and drove it away. When he returned, he had also filled up the tanks. Not only that, but he'd also filled the welder's tank that was on the trailer behind the truck.

I asked him why he'd done that. He replied, "Us Pentecostals are not about to be outdone by the Mennonites." I was utterly amazed at how the Lord blessed me that week with so much free fuel. I thanked God for His blessings and went home rejoicing that day.

Preaching the Sabbath Message

Laurence Gogol helped me for 22 years in my rototilling business.[3] He was good at estimating, so I often sent him to check out potential jobs and he was also good at running the rototiller. During the job we were doing for Eldon and Harold, he did the rototilling while I cleared the land with a CAT. Generally, at the end of each work day we would check in with the brothers to get a feel for what they wanted us to do the following day.

Inevitably, the conversation would turn to things of the Bible. They usually invited us in and we would converse about the Bible sometimes for hours. I gave them a copy of *The Desire of Ages*, which they read. After that they began keeping the Sabbath. I had left the CAT with them and allowed them to use it to clean up the land themselves. The brother became good friends of mine.

I spent a considerable amount of time completing jobs for Harold and Eldon. While I worked for them, I also got to know their older brother Ron. Ron was a kind-hearted and generous man and, after his brothers began keeping the Sabbath, he began to question me about my beliefs. One time he even urged me to come and speak at his church. "Please come and tell us what you believe," was his request.

I told him, "When I speak in front of a crowd, I get tongue-tied and I can't seem to think logically; everything I have to say just comes out sounding confused." Public speaking is one hurdle I've never really ever been able to master. I've been able to talk in front of others about my past experiences, but trying to communicate to a crowd about why I believe what I do is another matter entirely.

Still, Ron urged me to come and tell his church family what I believed. I told him I would see what I could do but the Lord worked it out for me that I could witness to the church family without setting foot in the church building. That year I did rototilling jobs for nearly every member of his church. And I was able to share my faith with each of them in a personal and intimate way. I've always found that witnessing one-on-one is the most effective way to share my faith.

All the same, after that whenever I saw Ron I felt sheepish for not going and doing as he had asked, begged really, and I even made efforts to avoid him whenever possible.

One day, the following winter, I decided to pay Harold and Eldon a visit. It was stormy, though, and the county had put in a new road which I was unfamiliar with. I got mixed up and couldn't seem to find their place. Just when I'd about given up looking, a truck came toward me from the opposite direction. Just before reaching where I was, it turned and ploughed into a snow bank. Thinking the driver might need help, I stopped to see if he or she was stuck. A man stepped out and, said, "Ben? What are you doing here?"

---

3   Missed dearly by me, he passed away in 2003 after a bout with cancer.

It was Ron. I was quite surprised and a little embarrassed to see him. I still felt guilty over not coming to talk to his church. "What are you doing out here in this weather?" I managed to ask then continued lamely, "You're not trying to get in that gate are you?"

"Honestly, Ben, I don't know what I'm doing here," he said in a confused tone of voice. "I bought this place a few months ago and haven't done anything with it yet. I drove here then realized I had no reason at all to be here and, after asking myself what on earth I was doing here, I decided to turn around, but then I accidentally swung into the gate. Strange that you'd be here at just the moment that I came by and did this," he mused. We stood quietly for a moment, considering the circumstances that had brought us together.

Then he said, "God must have led me here. Otherwise, I wouldn't have run into you. I've been wanting to talk with you about the Bible," he stopped a moment and kicked at the snow with the toe of his boot before continuing.

"You know that I'm the head elder at my Pentecostal Church and because of you, my two brothers are worshipping on Saturday," he toed the snow some more before looking up at me. "I want to know more about why they've changed."

It was 20° below zero and the snow was falling and blowing all around us. I kept my car running and we sat right there in the car and talked for at least an hour or more about Bible history and the Sabbath.

Chapter 11: Lay Evangelism Work

Three Hitchhikers: Two History Students and a Lutheran Minister

One day shortly after that, I was on my way to Calgary to pick up some parts. On my way home, I saw two young men hitchhiking. Much to the chagrin of my wife, picking up hitchhikers has always been one of my favourite things to do. I've never been able to pass one by without stopping to pick him or her up. Shirley used to say to me, "One of these days you'll pick up someone who makes you live to regret that you ever picked up a single hitchhiker."

It was a cold, wintry day and, of course, I stopped. They loaded their bags and got in. We introduced ourselves and I learned that they were History students at SAIT[1] and they were headed to Edmonton. I told them I wasn't going that far but I would take them as far as I could.

Minutes after I picked them up, they asked, "Do you mind if we smoke in your car?" I replied, "I'd rather you didn't because I don't smoke myself. However, there's a service station down the road about thirty miles. I was planning to stop there and get a bite to eat. You could have a smoke there while I've stopped."

"That's fine," they said, "This is your car. We're just glad for the ride." We had only driven a little way after that when we came upon another man hitchhiking. He only had a briefcase.

I stopped and he got in. He also said he was going to Edmonton. I told him that the other two boys were also going to Edmonton and asked where he was from. I believe he said he was from Illinois. He said he was a new minister, fresh out of a seminary in Missouri, and was headed to west Edmonton to take a Lutheran parish. We introduced ourselves all around then settled into a comfortable silence. A short while later, the minister took out a cigarette but didn't ask if I minded whether he smoked in my vehicle. "I'm sorry mister," I said politely, "I'd rather you didn't smoke in the car because I don't smoke myself. Cigarette smoke irritates my airways, but I'll be stopping soon. I promised these other two I'd stop so they could have a cigarette break. You can smoke then, too."

The two students who had been sitting quietly in the back were quite surprised by the minister's actions and began to question him. "You're a minister and you smoke?" The minister smiled sheepishly but appeared unable to answer the question. Then they turned

---

1   SAIT—Southern Alberta Institute of Technology located in Calgary, Alberta.

Chapter 11: Lay Evangelism Work

to me and asked, "Well Ben, what about you, you don't smoke? You seem like a nice guy. Are you a Christian?"

I answered, "I'm a Seventh-day Adventist. I believe that my body is the temple of the Living God and because smoking destroys people's bodies, I choose not to smoke." They responded, "That is so good. We wish we didn't smoke." Then they returned to questioning the minister. "Why do you smoke? You're a Lutheran and you're taking up the ministry. A minister should not smoke."

I thought they were pretty smart students. They were asking the questions I had wanted to ask him but didn't really feel comfortable enough to. I felt sure that he wouldn't be able to answer their questions because Lutheran clergy, as a general rule, are not taught about health and how being unhealthful creates barriers which prevent Jesus from being able to influence our intellects.

I decided to help him out of the hot seat and said, "Seventh-day Adventism isn't just a religion, it's a lifestyle. God's prescription for health and happiness is outlined in the Bible and I believe that those who follow it will get as close to the Eden experience as is humanly possible. Don't hassle him too hard," I told them. "Most Christians aren't even aware of these principles."

I explained that I believe my body is God's temple. In the Old Testament anything that would defile the Sanctuary (Temple) was not brought into it. Our bodies are much the same, so anything that would defile or destroy them should not be put into them. I told them that I make lifestyle decisions based on this principle. I explained that the Seventh-day Adventist Church does not advocate smoking, drinking alcohol, or eating unclean foods. Rather, a drug-free, vegetarian lifestyle, which involves drinking plenty of water, getting enough rest, exercise, fresh air and sunlight, and having faith in God, is encouraged.

"I follow this plan and that is why I don't smoke," I concluded. "Wow, we've never heard that before," they responded, "but it all makes sense. People shouldn't smoke, especially if they are going to be Christians!"

We began talking about other things when the Lutheran minister, who had been silent for quite some time, asked, "What else do Adventists believe?"

I told him, "We teach that Saturday is the Sabbath instead of Sunday." And then our conversation turned towards history. I tried to explain Nebuchadnezzar's dream from Daniel chapter two. We talked about Babylon, Medo-Persia, Greece, Rome, and Europe. The Lutheran minister disputed the order of what I was saying but the two in the back said, "Yes, that's right." From their history lessons, they knew this to be true. Of course I had my Bible with me and I gave it to the students in the back and the minister had his Bible as well. After reading Daniel, chapter two, the Lutheran minister, was dumb-founded. "This is really something," he said. "This is all of history in advance. This was written before there ever were any Romans or Greeks, etc." The two students also said, "This is really interesting."

We turned to other topics and again the minister spoke up and said, "I can't believe this! I've learned more today about Scripture than I did in the whole three years I spent in the seminary! I can't go and preach what they've taught me. At least not now that I know that what I've been taught isn't biblical. I'm going to have to change the direction of my life." I asked, "Why don't you become an Adventist minister?"

We had nearly approached my exit when he appealed, "Could we talk about this some more?" I exited the highway and pulled over to the side of the road before the end of the access lane where it would be safer for me to park the car. As the car idled, we sat and talked about the Bible and then we all prayed together. The two History students said they had decided to become Christians. They told me that if they had known that all these things were in the Bible, they would have become Christians long before. Learning of Bible prophecy in the book of Daniel had convinced them that the Bible was authentic and they wanted to follow what the Bible said. They thanked me for picking them up and teaching them about the Bible. It was after midnight and hitchhiking was difficult enough during the day. It was nearly impossible at night, so I made a quick decision and said to them, "I'm not going to let you hitchhike the rest of the way to Edmonton now on account of it being so late."

I drove them to their destinations. When I finally reached home, it was about 2:30 a.m. Shirley had been worried sick that something awful had happened to me, but after I related the events of that evening her heart was also filled with rejoicing. That was the last I saw of them and what became of them, I don't know. May God be with them. Certainly, rough times lay ahead for them and the Lord surely had to strengthen them. I look forward to seeing them in heaven.

Highways and Byways

And the lord said unto the servant, Go out into the highways and hedges, and compel them to come in, that my house may be filled. Luke 14:23

Another day as I was returning home from Calgary, I picked up a hitch-hiker. He was really sad. He looked like a lost sheep. I asked him, "Where are you going?" He said, "Edmonton." I asked, "Where are you going there?" He said, "The hostel."

Well I knew if he was going to the hostel, that's where he'd get something to eat and a place to stay. We talked a little while and he opened up to me. He said he'd just split up with his wife. He'd lost his home. He'd lost his job. Just everything went wrong. I told him, "You know, God can make things right." He said, "Oh, not the way she hates me."

I said, "God can change hearts, but He might have to change yours, too. God wants families to be together." I told him, "God is love. You just pray about it and let the Lord handle it for you." I said other things too over the two hours that we drove together. I took him to Olds and got him something to eat. I took him back to the highway and went to my home.

About six or eight months later I got a phone call. He called me and said, "I've been baptized and my wife's been baptized. We're members of your church now. And you know what? We're together now, happier than we've ever been. We got our place back and I've got a better job now than I had before."

I said, "Thank God! You surely made my day."

God Sends Me to Alix

I had been rototilling up north and when Sabbath came I was tired. My wife said, "You're going to rest today." That's just what I wanted to do. In the afternoon, I looked at some books and was relaxing, but then I started to get restless. My wife asked, "Why are you so restless?"

I said, "I've got to go."

She said, "You should rest. You've been working so much, you should rest."

I said, "I can't help it. I've got to go. I've got to give out books, or something. I've got to go."

I got in the truck and I moved the boxes of books that were on the seat. There were some *Desire of Ages* books and others. I drove to Alix and when I got to the end of a street I stopped and went to the house and knocked on the door. A woman answered and invited me in. I prayed, "Lord, I don't know what I'm doing here. Help me!"

The woman said, "I was praying that God would send you. If God hadn't sent someone, you see those pills over there?" She pointed at a bottle on the table. "I was going to commit suicide."

I told her God loves her and told her how lovely God is and that He died for our sins. I stayed awhile and we had a long talk. I prayed with her. She thanked me for coming and said, "God must have sent you." I felt He did, too.

After I left the woman's place, I was going to go straight home, but instead I ended up driving in the opposite direction, going north of Alix. There were two cemeteries on either side of the road. I saw a man standing by a fresh mound of earth. I went over to him and stood by him and asked, "Your wife?"

He said, "Yes, my wife."

I asked, "How long ago did she die?"

He said, "It's been a month now."

I said, "Was she a Christian?"

He said, "No. That's what's bothering me. She wasn't a Christian."

"Well, was she a good woman?" I asked.

He said, "Yes, she was a good woman. She was nice and honest and everything, but what bothers me so much is that she has to suffer so."

I said, "You mean, she *had* to suffer so?" I thought he meant she'd had a hard life.

He said, "No, you know what I mean. She wasn't a Christian."

I said, "You mean you think that she's down in hell and burning?" He nodded his head. "Don't believe that for a minute," I told him sternly. "That was the devil's first lie—that you don't die and that you go to hell and burn. God is love and He doesn't burn anybody forever and ever. The judgment day will come, but you can't judge that she'll be lost. Only God knows the heart and you don't. It's up to you just to live a good life and go to church. You just may meet again and have a big surprise because the Lord is loving."

He started to cry and gave me a big hug and he said, "God must have sent you." He cried until he soaked my shoulder. He said, "A great big load just lifted off me." He had spent thirty days just thinking that she was being tortured. What a doctrine, to make a God of love say that you'd have to be tortured with burning forever. It's sad that people teach that doctrine, but it's commonly preached in most churches today.

The Urgent, Still Small Voice

And thine ears shall hear a word behind thee, saying, This is the way, walk ye in it, when ye turn to the right hand, and when ye turn to the left. Isaiah 30:21

One Sabbath I was in church listening to Pastor Don Corkum. I was sitting in a pew at the left of the pulpit near the front and I felt a sudden urge to go. I never walk out on a pastor while he's preaching, but God urged me to go. I thought, How can I go? I wouldn't want people to think I didn't like the sermon. Pastor Corkum was a good speaker but something told me, "You've got to go. You've got to go." I believe it was God telling me to go.

I walked up to the front and out the side door. I was embarrassed that I had to sneak out on the sermon. I got into the truck and drove downtown and stopped at the middle of a block and walked up to a house and knocked on the door. A woman opened the door and said, "Come on in!"

I prayed, "Lord, help me."

She said, I was just praying that if God didn't send someone to me now, I wouldn't go back to church. I used to be an Adventist, but I stopped going about 50 years ago. I just prayed and now you're here. I'm going back next Sabbath." And she did.

A Financial Turn

Through those years, I had a good time financially. I helped a lot of students, helped a couple record their music, and supported the churches. But Solomon said, "Time and chance happen to us all." And so it happened to me. Things took a turn for the worse. It seems like when things happen, they don't happen singly, but they come in two's and three's.

Our house caught fire and inspectors figured it was a cigarette that started the fire in the basement. We had a renter in the basement, who wasn't supposed to smoke. We lost everything. The insurance didn't cover everything because we had a non-smoking policy.

My business was going strong, but I started a subdivision and things didn't go well. I'd sold some land to a fellow. He signed the legal papers and the money was in the Credit Union, but before my lawyer got over to take the money out, the purchaser went to the Credit Union, took the money and went and bought himself a big diesel truck and a car. When my lawyer went over to get the money, it wasn't there. So the buyer wound up with the money and title to the land.

Chapter 11: Lay Evangelism Work

Accidents and Injury

We built our next house on top of the one that burnt down. We still didn't have gas running to it, so I was heating the house with wood. I had a home-made wood-splitter. I shoved a block of wood on it and it slipped out of my hands and jumped cross-ways. The wood hit the side of my face, broke some bones and pushed my eye out of place. I had to rush to the hospital. The doctors pushed the bones back and pushed my eye through the temple. It bothered me a long time.

Next spring, I was working on a forklift in my yard. I was being careful because of the wood-splitter accident. I went to help Henry to prepare the forklift for moving, but I didn't know the two guys I'd hired to work with me had previously taken the chains off. I took a hammer and hit the forks and the whole mast of the forklift fell on me. The mast is the heavy vertical metal framework that the teeth slide up and down on. The whole assembly weighed about 4 000 pounds. As I fell, my head hit an anvil, knocking a hole in my skull behind my ear. The mast fell across my upper legs, torso and face. My arm and leg were crushed by it, but by the grace of God, the bones weren't broken. By another miracle, Henry got the thing off me and hauled me into the garage. An angel must have lifted it. It would have been impossible for one man to move 4 000 pounds of metal.

Henry thought I was dead. He started screaming and hollering. When I started coming around, I felt the back of my head and found a hole there. I grabbed an oily rag and shoved it into the hole to stop the blood from running onto the garage floor. My daughter came running out. She was nursing at the time and said, "Call an ambulance!"

I was rushed to Ponoka. My daughter wanted me to be sent to the university hospital in Edmonton. The doctor said, "No. We don't want to move him that far with his skull ripped up like that. I don't think he's going to make it. He'd never make it to Edmonton in this condition."

Miracles in the Operating Room

I passed out before the ambulance picked me up, but I started regaining consciousness when I arrived at the hospital. When I started coming round again, I tried telling the emergency workers about the hole above my ear, but no sound was coming out of my mouth. I could hear the workers talking, but I couldn't talk. I put my hand up to feel the hole, but it wasn't there. The hole was gone.

I was praying to God, "If only you keep me alive, I'll witness for you for the rest of my life. It isn't just for me, but for my grandchildren." We had two grandchildren and I said, "I don't want to leave them alone. It's not for my sake, but for their sake. Please spare my life." When I was praying, warmth came over me and I didn't have any pain.

Our pastor came to see me that night. He prayed with me and encouraged me. But I didn't see him the next day. He told me later, he didn't expect me to live through the night so he didn't come to the hospital the next morning. Nobody expected me to survive the night.

All night the doctor came and went. The nurse stayed with me constantly. The next morning the doctor came in and said, "Mr. Lippert, we never expected you to live till morning. But since you have, we've ordered Dr. McKean and Dr. McKay to come from Edmonton. They're here and we're going to put your skull back together. The bad thing is we're not going to give you any anaesthetic because we want you to be able to talk while we're working."

I said, "You go ahead. Twenty minutes ago I was praying because I was in such pain and now I haven't got a pain in the world." It was true. The Lord took away my pain and replaced it with a song, *My Jesus, I Love Thee*. It was one of Shirley's favourites and she often sang it.

The doctors had two trays of instrument that they had emptied from two suitcases. They drilled holes in the skull and used clamps to pull the bone into place and put my eye back where it belonged. While they worked on me the doctor said, "This is superhuman." He couldn't get over the fact that I was pain free. He walked to the wall and wept before he came back and finished the job. He kept saying, "This is supernatural. It's superhuman."

Chapter 12: My Weakness, God's Strength

Therefore I take pleasure in infirmities, in reproaches, in necessities, in persecutions, in distresses for Christ's sake: for when I am weak, then am I strong. 2 Corinthians 12:10

Two weeks later when I was home again, a man drove into the yard. He was interested in buying my business. My wife and I talked it over. With my health being what it was at that point, we started thinking maybe it would be a good idea to sell. We would keep the south quarter and he was going to give us a brand new mobile home to live in. He said, "I'll put you on easy street. You won't have to work." The way I was feeling I thought, That sounds okay.

The man offered to take us to Calgary to pick out a new mobile home. We stopped in Red Deer and looked at some mobile homes, then we went on to Calgary and looked some more. We saw one in Red Deer that had French doors and told him that was the one we'd like. He said, "I'll have it moved out for you."

We wanted to get things ready in the trailer after he'd taken over the business. He was working up in Athabasca with the machinery and he said, "Well don't make any changes right now. Don't touch that." I wondered, Why is he saying, "Don't touch that"?

Then we started learning the truth. We learned that the trailer hadn't been paid for. The buyer got it moved out to our place but never paid for it. We had trusted him. We tried to reach him by phone, but couldn't get hold of him. The bank told us that he'd lied about owning a lot of businesses. He just had the names down on paper, but they were all fictitious businesses. Meanwhile, he was racking up all kinds of charges against my business. The banker himself told us to file for bankruptcy. Over $200 000 worth of bills came pouring in and we had no idea where he was or how to reach him. I didn't even know where the equipment was.

The last we'd heard, he had been running the equipment around the Athabasca area about seven hours driving time from our home. So, I drove there to see if I could track him down and find the equipment. I was driving around Athabasca around four or five a.m., just as the sun was coming up. I thought I spotted something between the trees and went back through the bush and found the equipment, but it had been stripped. The engine was gone, the tires were gone. He sold everything off that he could. I went and asked a neighbour if I could store the equipment in his yard until I could arrange for transportation and he told me it would be alright.

The tractor and the rototiller needed months of repairs to get them in working condition. They both needed parts. I told my wife, "I've got to get another rototiller and get back to work. We've got payments to make." I sold off the acreages to pay the debt.

Miracle Window Money

I bought some land on the C&E Trail and vouched to pay so much per month until it was paid for. We moved into town for a while and worked from there and started to build on the land I'd bought. Money started to come in from some of the jobs, but it never seemed to be quite enough. We got the house framed up, but we didn't have any windows. I prayed, "Lord, we need to get some windows." I went to the local window shop and looked at all the windows. Someone had ordered a set of windows for $8 500 and never picked them up. The owner of the window shop said, "I'll sell them to you for $5 000 if you can use them." They were beautiful windows and would have been perfect for the house, but I had no money and the shop owner wouldn't sell the windows on credit.

It was Friday and I thought I'd clean up before the Sabbath. We had a lean-to on the trailer that we were living in. My daughter's kids were playing in there so I went in and started picking up the scattered toys. As I worked, my eyes fell upon a large envelope lying on the floor amongst the toys. I opened it and found $5 000, the exact amount I needed for the windows I'd seen that very day. What a miracle. Only God could have put that money there. The next week I went to the shop and bought the windows. The house is still there today and you can go and see the nice windows God blessed me with.

The Gospel Goes to a Grieving Family

> *But I would not have you to be ignorant, brethren, concerning them which are asleep, that ye sorrow not, even as others which have no hope.*
>
> *For if we believe that Jesus died and rose again, even so them also which sleep in Jesus will God bring with Him.*
>
> *For this we say unto you by the word of the Lord, that we which are alive and remain unto the coming of the Lord shall not prevent them which are asleep.*
>
> *For the Lord himself shall descend from heaven with a shout, with the voice of the archangel, and with the trump of God: and the dead in Christ shall rise first:*
>
> *Then we which are alive and remain shall be caught up together with them in the clouds, to meet the Lord in the air: and so shall we ever be with the Lord.*
>
> *Wherefore comfort one another with these words. 1 Thessalonians 4: 13-18*

One day while I was in the yard working on my rototiller, I had an urgent feeling that I must go somewhere at once. I had promised the farmer I was working for that I'd be at his farm the next morning and I wanted to finish repairing my equipment, so I resisted the Spirit's prompting. But the Spirit just kept speaking to me, "Go, go, go." The urge came stronger and stronger. Still I resisted. I was irritated. I didn't want to go. I wanted to work. Besides, I wasn't in any condition to visit. I was in my work clothes, covered with grease.

Chapter 12: My Weakness, God's Strength

But the urge was persistent. Finally, I grabbed my Bible and threw it on the truck seat. I don't remember starting the truck or driving. The next thing I knew, I was in Bentley on a side road facing uphill right in front of an old house.

I got out of the truck, grabbed my Bible and walked up the sidewalk to the house. I got halfway to the house and said, "God help me! I don't know why I'm here."

Just then a young lady came down the steps, moaning and crying. She came running to me and grabbed me and said, "Come in. We need you."

I went in, though I still didn't know what it was all about. There were seven or eight people in the room. I had never seen any of them in my life before. The girl who'd brought me in told me her brother had committed suicide just two hours before I got there. He was fifteen years old. She was sixteen.

The family told me that Dana[1] had been a good boy. He was always cheerful and happy and it was hard to understand why he committed suicide. Someone said, "He'd do anything for anybody." I told them that God knew his heart and there was hope that he might be in heaven. I encouraged the family to go to church and get to know Jesus.

They asked me how I knew about the suicide. "Why did you come?" they asked. I said, "I didn't know about the suicide and I don't know why I came. I just felt I had to come here."

One of the relatives said, "That's unreal. Are you real?" He came over and pinched me. He just couldn't understand that God had sent me to them. Perhaps the Ethiopian pinched Philip, too. (See Acts 8.)

I stayed with them several hours and told them I had to go home and get the rototiller ready for tomorrow morning. Candace, Dana's sister, the girl who'd brought me into the house, said she was not leaving me. "I'm going with you," she said. I didn't know if she meant permanently or what. I took her along and drove the long way home and told her to let it out if she felt like crying.

I had to stop the truck a couple of times because she was so emotionally overwhelmed. It was risky driving when she went into these fits because she was holding onto me and shaking so hard from the crying. What hurt her especially about her brother's death, she told me, was that he had called her an hour before he committed suicide, but she had told him she couldn't come right then. The guilt was tearing her apart. I had wet shoulders when I got home she cried so much.

The Unbearable Weight of Guilt

Guilt is an awful weight to bear. It really can destroy a person. That is why Jesus said, "Take my yoke upon you, and learn of me; for I am meek and lowly in heart: and ye shall find rest unto your souls. For my yoke is easy, and my burden is light." (Matthew 11:30) Jesus wants us to roll our burden of sin and guilt onto Him. He died to release us from the crushing burden, once the guilt has done its appointed work. Guilt's job, according to 2 Corinthians 7:10 is to bring us to repentance. "For godly sorrow worketh repentance to

---
1 Name has been changed.

salvation not to be repented of: but the sorrow of the world worketh death."

I never saw Candace or her family again. I drove out to the house some time later, but the family had moved. I can only pray that her burden of guilt moved her to seek God. I pray that she turned her life over to Him and let Him remove that sorrow from her heart. I will look for her and her brother in Heaven.

Hit and Run

One day, I took Shirley to Lacombe. She had a medical appointment and we had to sign the papers on a house we were buying in Alix. Shirley was usually an hour or an hour and a half at the doctor's so this day I decided to leave the car at the hospital and walk over to the store and do our grocery shopping.

When I got to a cross walk, a big car was in the intersection with a little car behind it. The big car drove off, but the little car didn't move, so I started to cross. Just when I got in front of the car, the woman at the wheel stepped hard on the accelerator. The car hit me and spun me around. The wheel went over my foot. The impact wrenched my back and tore ligaments in my shoulder. I lay on the pavement for a moment, hardly able to move. The car sped away. I managed to get up and get to the lawyer's office to sign the papers for the house. The lawyer looked at me and said, "What's the matter with you?" I said, "I just got hit by a car and I hurt my back." The lawyer started writing. He said, "You go to the police and report it." So I filed a report with the police. Then I went to the chiropractor to get some help for my back. He worked on me and oh, my back was sore.

After that, whenever I walked, my right leg would give out and I'd fall down. I fell on my elbow and hurt my elbow. Another time, I was standing and talking with someone when my leg just buckled. I fell so hard, my neck cracked. The guy said, "What's the matter?" I said, "I don't know. Ever since that accident, my right leg just gives out and I fall."

"Well, you'd better get that checked," advised my friend.

I told the lawyer about what was happening. He sure wasn't the lawyer for me. It cost me $10 000 and I got no restitution. I suffered a lot and couldn't work.

About that time, we realized we would have to move to Ponoka. Shirley's doctors said, "You'd better get her close to a hospital." We moved to our present home, so the nurses could come and help Shirley, because I couldn't do all the work due to my injuries.

Meanwhile, my wife's medical treatments were running up bills. One medication alone cost $75 per pill. I was making trips to Edmonton trying to get the government to pay for that pill. I filled out a lot of forms. I wouldn't hear from the medical authorities for a long time, and then they'd turn me down. In Ponoka, the medical expenses reached $1 100 each month.

At one point, the strain was finally just too much for me. My wife's failing health, constant worry over our financial troubles, and my accident were more than I could cope with. I had a breakdown and ended up in the hospital very, very sick.

I had been planning to take Shirley to the hospital because she wasn't well and in a

Chapter 12: My Weakness, God's Strength

lot of pain. I wasn't feeling well myself. I started getting sick on Wednesday and she was supposed to be in the Lacombe hospital on Friday. That Friday I was driving her to the hospital and I was so weak, that it looked to me like the road was moving. I stopped the car and fell out of the door and put my head down. I had excruciating pain in my legs like there were bands of iron around my bones. Somehow I made it to the hospital. I drove into the ambulance bay and opened the door and fell out. The workers came and got me and put me in bed.

At first the doctor thought I had leukemia. I was so sick I was ready to call my loved ones together. I didn't think I could live through another night. I was so weak I couldn't even lift my head up anymore. The nurses dressed me and carried me on a stretcher to the ambulance to transport me to Red Deer. I was just about in the ambulance when the doctor came running out calling, "Don't go! Don't go. I got a call from the university." It turned out I was given the wrong diagnosis. It wasn't leukemia, but pernicious anaemia. They started giving me B12 injections. In two days, after giving me shots, I was back on my feet again. However, because of the mistaken diagnosis, my hands became crippled and I have constant pain due to the irreparable nerve damage in my arms and legs. Sometimes I feel like I've got metal bands on my legs above and below the knees. It's an awful feeling. Still, God has been very good to me.

Shirley was in the same hospital in another room, but unlike me, she didn't get better. She kept getting worse. We got our daughter to move to the basement because she's a nurse and would know what to do if Shirley passed out. The basement wasn't a very good place. It was pretty homely with its six-foot ceiling and being unfinished as it was. The county sent home-makers out to help with Shirley's care, but she spent more time in the hospital than she did at home.

Unwell but Working

Things became very rough financially while we were in Ponoka. Bills kept piling up. I wasn't well, but I told my wife, "I'm going to have to go and buy a rototiller. I've got to do something to make some money." I heard about one for sale and it turned out to be the tractor and rototiller I used to have years ago. I had sold it to this guy's father, so I made a deal with the man over the phone, though I hadn't even looked at it. The son told me he'd put $50 000 into it recently. He told me everything was new and the engine was good and the rear end was good and everything else was good, too. I just took his word for it because I was too sick to drive out and look at it and I had known his dad and trusted him. I didn't know the son was different from his father.

Little did I know you couldn't even steer the tractor. I had to borrow money again and gave the guy $15 000 down and we made up a contract. I hooked up my little car behind because I was going to drive the tractor home towing the car. I went to drive it out of the yard, and I couldn't even steer it. It just went jerk, jerk, jerk. The whole steering pump was all haywire, the alternator didn't work and the battery was going dead. It was getting dark and I was up on the busy Trans Canada Highway, near Banff.

At 2 a.m., after a lot of trouble, I got to Cremona. I parked the tractor and rototiller at a parking lot next to a hotel and went home, still a three hour drive from Cremona. The next day I went back to Cremona and got to work on the machinery. I was in a hurry to get it going because I had to make a dollar. It took me a week just to get it running. I had to fix the tractor and everything was wrong with the rototiller.

I worked on the rototiller in Cremona for about a month. I had nothing but trouble, but I believe God put me there for a reason. The town drunk lived in a truck in the same parking lot where I was working on the machinery. I talked with him as he went back and forth. Sometimes he stood and watched me work.

My first priority was to get the machinery in decent running condition. The next thing was to get it looking presentable. The tractor and the rototiller both looked awful. They were dented and had rust spots. The paint was faded, scratched and chipped. I bought some spray paint in cans and did a rough paint job. The drunk wasn't around most of that day. When he showed up, he said to me, "I'm right out of money. I'm a painter. I could have painted your rototiller for you." I had done an ugly job of painting the thing, alright.

I said, "I'd like my phone number painted on it." He said, "I'll do it for you for nothing." He went and got a can of black paint out of his truck and put my phone number on the machine.

The hardware store owner heard that he was hard up and he told me to tell him to come in and he'd give him the paint and the brushes and he could paint the east wall of the hardware store for $50. So I told this fellow and he was happy to do it.

Everlasting Punishing?

After he got paid, the drunk went to the liquor store and bought a case of beer and something else that he carried in a paper bag. He came walking by me just as a couple of guys drove up to see me. One fellow in the truck yelled out his open window, "You're going to burn forever in hell!"

I turned to the drunk who was walking by on the sidewalk, "God would never do a thing like that. God loves you." The drunk didn't stop. He kept on walking.

The fellows got out of the truck and said, "You're a religious man. Don't you believe the Bible?"

"Yes, I believe the Bible. I just don't believe in eternal hell," I told them.

They said, "But the Bible says, 'everlasting punishment'."

"Yes," I said, "but it doesn't say 'everlasting punishing.'" They shook their heads as they thought about it. "Everlasting punishing" goes on, but "everlasting punishment" comes to an end at some point. It's over.

They really appreciated that explanation. "That's nice to know," they told me. I guess that bothered some of those people a lot and I wonder how many others worry about what happens to the unsaved at the end of time. The Bible has the truth about the judgment and hell, but many are confused about this doctrine because they have been deceived by God's enemy.

Chapter 12: My Weakness, God's Strength

Satan's first lie to Adam and Eve was "Ye shall not surely die." (Genesis 3:4). This is a direct contradiction of what God said. "The soul that sinneth, it shall die." (Ezekiel 18:4) In 2 Thessalonians 1: 7-9 the Bible speaks about the final, or everlasting, destruction of the wicked in these words:

When the Lord Jesus shall be revealed from heaven with His mighty angels, In flaming fire taking vengeance on them that know not God, and that obey not the gospel of our Lord Jesus Christ: Who shall be punished with everlasting destruction from the presence of the Lord, and from the glory of His power.

Of Jesus John the Baptist said, "Whose fan is in His hand, and He will thoroughly purge His floor, and gather His wheat into the garner; but He will burn up the chaff with unquenchable fire." (Matthew 3:12) Chaff that is burned up doesn't exist anymore. All that is left are ashes. And though no human being will be able to stop the fire of judgement that God starts, once the fuel for the fire has been consumed, the fire will go out on its own. Otherwise, what kind of paradise could the redeemed enjoy if they knew their loved ones who had rejected God were being tortured forever by Him? Satan invented the doctrine of everlasting punishing to make God look bad and hateful rather than loving and merciful. Many people, Christians included, suffer untold anguish over these deceptions.

Chapter 13: Faith that Moves Mountains

But my God shall supply all your need according to His riches in glory by Christ Jesus. Philippians 4:19

It was a 125 mile (200 km) trip each way from our home to Cremona. I got pretty sick and was feeling too faint to work, so I couldn't make it back for a while. I told Shirley, "I'm just not feeling well." After a week or so, I returned and loaded the tanks with fuel. I wasn't well enough to work, but I told my wife I'd fuel up the equipment, grease it and get it ready to go for when I felt better. On the way there, the tire cap on the right rear wheel flew off, tearing off plastic from the fender.

"I can't fix it," I thought. It was hot and the heat just made me feel so weak and faint. I pulled into the town of Olds and asked around for a tire shop. A fellow told me there was one right near the railway tracks. I got there, but I knew I didn't have any money to pay for the repairs. I told the repairman that the front wheels would have to go on the back, because I didn't have a spare and the rear wheels had to match. He understood and got to work. He was just sweating away trying to remove the bolts because I think the tires were the original ones that came with the truck. It was an old truck, but I don't think the tires had ever been changed and the bolts were rusted on tight. I was watching them work and thinking about what it was going to cost me. I figured maybe they had done at least $100 worth of work, but I didn't have that much.

I went to the office when the tire was fixed, but instead of coming in and writing my bill, the fellow just went over to the shop and started working on another tire. I said, "Sir, I'd like to get squared up with you. I'm in a bit of a hurry, because I'd like to get to Cremona before dark."

"We're not taking any money from you," he said. "We've heard about you and we know what you've done. You go ahead and enjoy yourself." To this day, I don't know what he meant.

I drove back to Cremona to fuel up the rototiller and grease it. After I greased it up and fueled up the tractor and rototiller I unlocked the door. There was an envelope that someone had shoved through the crack under the tractor door. Inside the envelope were twelve twenty dollar bills and a note that said, "For what you've done for us. God bless you." I was dumbfounded. Who could have done this? I wondered. It refreshed my spirit and made me feel healthier even. The Word of God tells us in Proverbs 17:22, "A merry heart doeth good like a medicine: but a broken spirit drieth the bones." It's really true. I

Chapter 13: Faith that Moves Mountains

praised the Lord for the gift.

The kindness of the tire shop fellows and the money in the cab cheered me up so much I decided to go and finish the job I'd started about a month before. At that time, I had done some work for a family in Cremona and had about six hours to complete. I worked on the field the first day and the next morning I drove to the field, climbed up the tractor steps and unlocked the door. A little while later, the farmer whose field I was working on drove over on his trike, a three-wheeled all-terrain vehicle (ATV).

I asked, "Who put this envelope in my tractor?"

"I'm not telling you anything," was his answer.

I tried to guess but he stayed true to his word and wouldn't tell me who'd done it. I would have liked to have known who did it because I really wanted to thank that person or persons. I was under such stress trying to pay the bills that having that gift of money just made my day.

Once the farmer left, I looked at the work ahead of me and thought I could probably finish the job in about five or six hours, if I didn't have any difficulties. The only problem was there was a big slough on the field. The trouble with sloughs is, it isn't always easy to tell where the soft, wet soil ends and the firm, dry soil begins. I dreaded getting stuck because I was too sick to deal with that. I was praying, "Lord, I don't want to do the slough. I'm scared to do the slough because I'm likely to get stuck in there."

Each round brought me nearer the slough. Then I saw the farmer walking out to see me. He said, "Ben, my wife and I have been thinking about that slough. We feel it's just a waste of money to have to do that. Would you mind not rototilling the slough?"

"Oh, I don't mind," I told him cheerfully, thanking God at the same time. "I'm not feeling well anyway."

"Alright," he said. "As soon as you're done, come on in and we'll square up."

When I finished, I told the farmer he owed me $1 600 and he wrote me a cheque for $1 800. I said, "No, it's $1 600."

The man's wife came out of the kitchen and said, "Ben, I wanted to give you $100 personally and George wanted to give you $100, too. You're working hard and you're not well, we can see that. Besides, you go to church and you tell people about God. You even tell us. You've been an inspiration to us. If we were rich, we'd give you more. But we want to thank you for what you have done, so you take it." Well, I did and I thanked them very much and I became close friends with them.

That day I felt that God fulfilled His promise in Deuteronomy 28:2 where it says, "And all these blessings shall come on thee, and overtake thee, if thou shalt hearken unto the voice of the LORD thy God." He certainly sent His blessings on before me that day.

Money in the Mail

A good name is rather to be chosen than great riches, and loving favour rather than silver and gold. Proverbs 22:1

About this same time, Shirley was very sick and not doing well at all. She'd had a knee replacement done and it turned out bad and her bone split. She had a lot of pain because of that. Every few days I'd have to take her to the doctor for one reason or another. Her blood pressure was so high, she'd have headaches. On top of all the physical suffering, the cost of medical care was putting us deeper and deeper into debt. Things went on this way for several years.

Around 6 o'clock one night I was praying to the Lord about Shirley's suffering and our looming debt. It was costing me $250 for one week's worth of medicine. I said, "Lord, I can't turn any more. I've sold everything. I can't pay this."

I got up from praying and the phone rang. The guy on the phone said, I don't know how to put it, but I'm looking for a man—he's kind of a preacher/rototiller man."

"Well, I've never been called that before," I told him, "But I suppose that describes me pretty well."

He said, "Could I have your name and address?"

I said, "Where are you from?" he said "Caroline" That's way down south of Rocky Mountain House, about 125 miles from my home. I hadn't been there in thirty years or so. The caller's name was Chris Hawn and I didn't know him. He'd asked for my address and I didn't know why. I gave him my address and three or four days later a cheque for $250 arrived in the mail. That was exactly what I needed for that week's medical expenses.

I had his phone number on the cheque so I called him and asked, "What's this cheque about?"

He said, "The Holy Spirit instructed me to send it."

"Well, why me?" I asked.

"Well, Ben," he said, "the reason I sent that is because you got my two best friends going back to church again."

After that, we called each other from time to time and started having prayer on the phone together, but I hadn't ever met him. The highest amount he sent me was $700. Finally, about a month and a half before my wife passed away I told her, "I've got to meet this man. I'm going to go down there." I went to the town of Caroline and got directions to his place.

When I got there, there was nobody there. I didn't know they were back in the woods with a skidoo hauling fire wood. I took out the book, *God's Gift to Modern Man*. I was going to write a note and thank him for all he'd done. Then I heard the sound of the snowmobile coming from the bush. A woman was driving with a sleigh full of fire wood hooked up behind. I walked up to the woman and said, "I'm Ben Lippert." She came running toward me and gave me a hug just as if she knew me all her life. She said, "We've been praying for you! God answered our prayers!" She seemed really excited, but I didn't know why.

Chapter 13: Faith that Moves Mountains

I helped her unhook the sled and she said, "Oh, Chris is going to be happy." Then she took off on the snowmobile back toward the bush. She was going so fast, I thought she might hit a tree. They came back quickly and walked one on either side of me. They said, "Come on into the house."

We got into the house and she had two apple pies that she'd just baked in the wood stove. I had dinner with them. I gave them *God Speaks to Modern Man* and we talked about the Bible. That's all we ever talked about the whole time, just the Bible.

When it started getting dark I said, "Well, I've got to go." And I was watching that they didn't write a cheque. I didn't want them to think I'd come out because I wanted their money. Lori said, "Couldn't you stay longer?"

I said, "No, my wife is pretty sick and I want to get back before 8:30."

She said, "Well, take the other pie."

I said, "No, I couldn't do that. It's the only one you've got left."

But they insisted. Chris grabbed a plastic bag and Lori put the pie into it and tied the bag with a knot and handed it to me. "It's a present for you," he said. I thanked them and had a little prayer and asked God's blessing upon them. I said goodbye and away I went, but I felt like I was in heaven. That's how I felt, because it was such a joy to have Christian fellowship with people who loved God the way I did.

I got to the hospital and went to see my wife and told her what nice people I'd visited with and that we'd talked about the Bible the whole afternoon. "And they sent an apple pie along," I told her.

Shirley said, "Go out and get it. Maybe I could eat a little bit of it. I went and brought the pie and my daughter came in and undid the knot because I was having trouble with it. She pulled out the pie and along came an envelope with it. Marlene said, "Dad, here's $500."

I said, "When in the world did they write that cheque? I was watching and I didn't see them write that cheque."

When I got home that night I phoned and said, "Lori, I came down to visit you and I didn't intend to get any money. I just wanted to get to know you because you people have been so good to me. How did that cheque get in there? I didn't see you guys write it."

She said, "Ben, we wrote the cheque the day before. We were going to mail it, but we thought, No. Let's pray that Ben comes down instead."

"Oh!" I said. "Now I know why you said, 'You answered our prayers.' You prayed last night that I'd come and today I came."

She said, "Yes! You answered our prayers."

I thought, what people! They had that much faith in God to believe that I'd come and visit them just because they prayed.

I told her, "I'd like to put this $500 cheque on the wall for a souvenir."

She said, "No, Ben. We want you to have it to pay your medical bills. We don't have any kids and besides our stocks went up three times since we started helping you. We've been blessed by you."

So, I did cash it and paid the medical bills. They followed right through until my wife passed away in March, 2004.

We still talk to each other. When I felt that I would be crushed by the mountain of debt I was under, God sent Chris along to help move that mountain. God answers prayers so mysteriously and has so many ways of meeting our needs, we can't even imagine what they might be. We only need to trust Him and have faith. Jesus said, "For verily I say unto you, That whosoever shall say unto this mountain, Be thou removed, and be thou cast into the sea; and shall not doubt in his heart, but shall believe that those things which he saith shall come to pass; he shall have whatsoever he saith." (Mark 11: 23) No mountain is too great for the Lord to move for us when we have faith.

Chapter 14: More Faith that Moves Mountains

If ye have faith as a grain of mustard seed, ye shall say unto this mountain, Remove hence to yonder place; and it shall remove; and nothing shall be impossible unto you. Matthew 17:20

A guy phoned me one night and asked me to come and rototill twenty acres of brush that he cleared the previous year. I asked, "Where do you live?"

He told me, "Near Gadsby. Two miles south, a mile west and a quarter mile south."

I said, "That's our old farm. We lived there back in the '40's!"

He said, "Oh! It would be interesting then if you came. You could tell me a lot about this place." I told him I'd be out there Monday. I got there late, because it was a long way to drive, about 100 miles (160 km) from my home.

We got talking about the place. They had torn the porch off the house. There had been coloured glass in the door and I asked what they had done with the door. They had saved the door, they told me. It was sitting in the chicken coop and we went over and looked at the coloured glass. We went to the barn and they showed me the bars where we had fastened our cows for milking.

I started rototilling, but it got to be evening soon after and I had to stop for the day. I met with the farmer and told him I had a story for him about when I had lived there. I told him the story about how my mom and I got into arguments.

I told him, "I was always mad because mom would throw my sins at me all the time. She told me, 'You're always angry!' But she was the one that made me angry. I guess I should take half the blame."

I said, "It got so hot between us one day, I was mad at God. Mother told me my sins were piled up to heaven. I went right over there to where there was an ash pile," I said, pointing to the spot in the barnyard.

The farmer said, "Yes, I remember the ash pile there. We hauled it away."

"It was sunset on Friday evening," I continued. "I went out to the ash pile and I didn't know what I was going to say to God, but I wanted Him to kill me, so I wouldn't have any more sins piling up. I looked over to the sunset and suddenly, I had a feeling just like something warm had wrapped around me. I just felt a sweet peace, something so nice, I can't explain it. There are no words to describe it. I just started to cry. I stayed there and watched the sun set till it disappeared. Then I went to the house and told Mom, 'I know God loves me.' She said, 'Yes, Benny. I agree.' And she started crying and we hugged each other and forgave each other."

By the time I finished the story, the couple were crying. They told me they wanted to be Christians too. I talked Bible to them a long time and gave them some books and videos. They gave their lives to Christ. I visited often with them after that. I still visit with them to this day.

When I had finished my work for the farmer he said, "I bought a rocky quarter just down the road a way, would you mind taking a look at it with me?" I said, "You know rocks and rototillers don't go well together."

He said, "I'll help move the rocks out of the way."

To be a gentleman, I said, "Alright. Let's get on with it." The property was about five miles (8 km) away. We drove over I looked at it. It was full of rocks, big and small. I said, "Oh, you'll need a front-end loader with teeth to lift these rocks out." He assured me he and his wife would take care of it. "We'll do that," he told me.

So I took the job on, but I was not feeling well. I was developing sugar diabetes at the time and didn't know it. I started on a Wednesday and worked through Thursday. On Friday they came and told me that they were leaving to attend a wedding up north about 700 miles (1 126 km) away in Peace River. They wanted to know if I could manage finishing the rest of the work myself. Like a dummy, I said, "Yes." I didn't want to say, No, anyway because I didn't want to spoil their going to the wedding. They said they wouldn't be back till Monday.

Since it was Friday and I don't work Saturdays, I went home and I was feeling really rough. I stayed home Sabbath, then Sunday morning I screwed up my courage to get back to Gadsby and finish the job. I didn't know if I should even get out of bed, because I was feeling kind of faint. I drove halfway to the farm, all the while wondering whether I should turn around and go back home. I rested for a while and prayed and continued on my way.

I fuelled up the machinery and thought maybe I'd do a round or two. So I started to go around. I had to jump off the tractor once or twice each round to move rocks. It was five feet to the seat of the tractor from the ground and each time I jumped down and climbed back up again, I had to sit awhile to clear my head before continuing with the work. I was really suffering. But I felt good about what I had done for the people. I had brought them to Christ. I felt good spiritually, but I was sick physically.

I was getting close to a big rock. It was more like a boulder, really. The part that stood above ground was about a foot and a half tall and more than two feet wide. It was a giant of a rock and I worried about having to move it. I figured I'd have to get a bar and pry it and try to roll it off. That would be difficult, because my fingers are weak and don't work well because of the pernicious anaemia. I just wasn't feeling strong enough.

I knew I would come to the rock in the next round. I just said to the Lord, "I'm so tired, I just can't go on." But I was desperate to work to make enough money to pay my wife's medical bills.

I came to the end of the round and was driving and driving, waiting for that rock. I kept looking for it, though I knew I couldn't possibly miss it. The field isn't that big and there's only one approach to it. I came to where I thought the rock should be in relation to the approach, but there was no rock. I went around again and I was thinking, "Where's that rock?" It wasn't there.

"Thank you, Jesus!" I cried out. I don't know what He did with that rock, whether He threw it into the lake or what. Well, I finished the round and kept on working and never picked up a single stone after that. Every time I drove by where I thought that rock should have been, I always got a feeling that God's presence was there. I finished the whole field, got in the vehicle and drove home.

The Curse of Self-Sufficiency

Humble yourselves in the sight of the Lord, and He shall lift you up. James 4:10

Not long ago, the church had a bunch of books in one of the rooms. Some of them were ten years old already. Pastor David Beaudoin said, "We've got all these books and nobody to give them out." Mark Finley's *Thirteen Reasons* was there and others as well.

I said, "I can't carry much because my arm is bad, but if you get them out to my car I'll pass them out." The church was planning on holding an evangelistic series that fall. They put several boxes of books in the trunk. So I went door-to-door from morning to night.

I came to the first door and when a man opened it, I held out a book and said, "I'm just giving out free books." He said, "Oh, it's religion, eh?" And he gave it back to me quickly.

I prayed, "Lord, help me."

Then I said, "What denomination are you?"

"I don't go to church," he said.

I kept talking and I don't remember what I said, but I got a conversation going. I told him how the book changed my life. I told him I even thanked God for my heart attack because I probably never would have read that book if I hadn't had a heart attack. He was impressed by that. He reached over and grabbed the book out of my hand and said, "I'm going to read it now." He's the only guy who did that to me.

Then I had my worst day. You know, we sometimes get to a place where we think we're pretty good at something and we forget to pray. We tend to forget that it's God's leading that helps us give out books.

This one morning I had packed up two boxes of books. There were 80 books in each box. I put them in the truck. I had covered all the little towns in the area but the town where our Adventist college is. I figured there were too many Adventists there. So I decided go east and cover the territory right up to the Saskatchewan border, which is about three hours away from where I started. I did 25 miles (40 km) in every direction.

That morning I started up to the first place. There was a guy riding a lawn tractor. He shut it down and I told him, "I'm giving out for free a book that changed my life."

"Religion!" he shouted. He hollered at me to get off his blankety, blank property right now. I got in the car and drove off. I was pretty shaken up.

Instead of praying, I drove up to the next farm. I got another rebuke just about as bad. I drove out of there feeling really shaken up. I turned off the road and parked on an approach to a farm field. I just bowed my head and said, "Lord, I'm sorry. I forgot to pray. It's your work, not mine. I'm just your servant. Please bless me today and forgive my thought of who I am and that I can do this."

God forgave my presumptuousness. He poured out His grace upon me and filled me with courage. I went out on the road again, this time in the Lord's strength, not in my pride. And the Lord turned that day into a blessing.

I'll never forget that day. I stopped at the home of a Catholic woman. I told her what I was doing and before I could offer to pray for her, she said, "Could I pray for you?"

"Yes, that would be nice," I said. It wasn't often that someone offered to pray for me. She prayed the nicest prayer and asked God to bless me for giving out those books. What a nice lady.

From there I went to another place where we used to live and I drove up to McArthur's farm. Mr. McArthur himself was still living in the house and he came to the door and said, "There was a family who lived in the Winslett place back in '41. They were Adventists. I'd like to know where they are. I got sick and I was down for several months and this Fred, he came down every day and did the chores."

He didn't know that was my family he was talking about and Fred was my father.

"They put up hay for me," he said. "I thought they were well off but I didn't know that they didn't even own their own farm." He said, "I wanted to thank them. They had a son that came along who milked the cows. His name was Ben, I think."

"Do you mean the Lipperts?" I asked.

"Yes," he said, brightening.

I said, "You're looking at Ben."

He gave me a big hug. I told him that Dad passed away just a few years earlier.

"Oh, I'm sorry," he said. He hugged me again and cried on my shoulder. He said, "If ever there was a man of God, it was your dad."

Then I went to another place and they were just so friendly. The people invited me in and said, "You've got to come in. You've got to eat."

I told them about Christ and how the *Desire of Ages* had changed my life. I told them that when I read that book in the hospital, I had wept half the night not because I was sad but because what I read in there about God's love for us was so beautiful.

"We want the book," they said.

I came home late. It was almost 11 p.m. As I was driving west toward home, I could see the sunset and I just felt the peace of God. I felt like I was in heaven. It was such a nice feeling. God surely blessed me. But I had to get knocked down a couple of times before I could be lifted up.

Chapter 15: Ripples on the Water

I did some work for a couple who lived north of my place. They were so nice, but the husband was gone a lot. The wife, Debbie[1], would run and open gates for me. I said, "You don't have to do that, Debbie."

"I get tired in the house," she told me. So I let her help by opening the gates. It saved me having to climb up and down the tractor ladder.

The couple had two kids. Their girl was fourteen and she stayed out at other people's places. Debbie worried a lot about her children. She said, "I have no control over the kids. Gerald's gone so much and I don't know how to deal with the kids half the time."

She often asked me to have dinner with her so she wouldn't feel so alone. I think she just needed someone to talk to because she told me about her problems. I guess she felt pretty lonely, because she said they didn't have any friends nearby. One day she said, "Gerald and I consider you our best friend."

I told her about the Lord and that He loves them. We ended up having such a nice relationship. She gave me $900 more than what I'd asked for. When I insisted on giving it back, she said, "Oh, no, Ben. We want you to have that. We just really appreciate you coming. Our life has been changed." I thanked her.

Then she said, "We've decided we need to do something about going to church."

I really wanted to tell her to go to our church not far from their home, but I was scared because they had told me about some trouble they'd had because of a couple of the church members I knew attended that church. I didn't know how to put it and it scared me to say, "Well go there anyhow." I ended up not recommending a church and I felt so bad, because I couldn't ask them to go to our church.

We often don't realize how far-reaching our influence can be, I think. How many more people would be in the church if only we would remember that our reputation in the community and in the church either honours the Lord or dishonours Him? James 2:7 says, "Do not they blaspheme that worthy name by the which ye are called?" Let us always remember that our influence can either build up God's church or tear it down. Let us strive to never be a stumbling block to those whom Christ died for.

I still visit with this couple from time to time and share Christian books with them.

After that, I moved over to the neighbour's farm a mile across from Gerald's and Debbie's farm. What a nice guy the neighbour was. He was kind of rough and used a lot of foul language. I often reminded him, "God loves you." It's funny, but it seems that bad

---

1   Name has been changed.

language and dirty jokes need audience participation. I've found that by refusing to laugh or swear along with people who do those things, they often clean up their acts. That is just what happened with that fellow. His language straightened out while I was there. I saw such a change in him those few days, it was remarkable. He talked differently and seemed to like to be close to me. He'd bump me as he walked by. I think he felt God's presence.

I told him, "God loves you. Live the best you can with God's help." I shared some of the doctrines with him, also. Then I moved on to another job.

Too Busy for God

One young farmer I worked for was in a rush. During the three or four days that I worked for him, I noticed that whenever he was around his family, he was uptight. He was snappy and didn't treat his wife or his children right. He was under such tension.

One day, I took him aside and said, "Dan, I'm just trying to give you a little help in your life. The good Lord says don't worry about tomorrow. It will take care of itself. Just slow down and think of your children and be nice to them. They grow up so fast and you'll find yourself sitting all alone. Enjoy them while they're young and speak nicely to them and to your wife. There are too many broken homes already."

His head dropped a little nearer to his chest, but he listened quietly.

I said, "The good Book says to enjoy life. Whatever you do, do it with all your might and enjoy it. It's a gift from God."

He nodded and thanked me for telling him this. He called a week or so later and said, "Ben, we'd like to come over and visit with you."

Instead, I went over and visited with them and gave them some Adventist books. We became good friends.

Abortion

Lo, children are an heritage of the LORD: and the fruit of the womb is His reward. Psalm 127:3

When we moved to Ponoka, I was so sick I wasn't much help, but the local church folks moved all our stuff for us. Thank God for church folks. It was the nicest move we ever made. I never moved into a town and made so many friends so quickly.

It wasn't just church members who were friendly, either. I developed friendships with many of the store workers I dealt with, too. One of them was a young clerk at the drugstore. I had to go to the drugstore quite frequently, sometimes two or three times a day, so I got to know the workers quite well. The young clerks were always so nice.

One Sunday morning I was lying in bed. Shirley was in the hospital, so I was alone. Suddenly, I heard a roar coming up the back alley. There was an old Chevy 4 x 4 truck with a girl waving out the window. I went outside and it was the girl who worked in the drugstore. She was with her boyfriend. I said, "It's so nice that you came to see me." She

Chapter 15: Ripples on the Water

gave me a big hug. They told me every Sunday she and her boyfriend Jake would go out for drives. He'd asked her, "Where do you want to go this Sunday?" She said, "I want to go see Ben." Then she said, "I'm pregnant." She was only sixteen. She said, "Jake and I were talking about an abortion. But I said I wasn't going to do anything till I talk to Ben."

I told her, "No way. You don't have an abortion. That's not the way. You'll always wonder what the baby looked like." I encouraged her to return to her parents on the east coast. So, she did. She was away for over a year and then she returned. She called me when she got back to town and I went to see her. She thanked me for the advice I'd given her. "I'd never give up my baby," she said. She left her boyfriend. "He was a bit of a rascal," she told me. She's got a good job now and the child is doing well.

Sent With an Encouraging Word

Therefore encourage one another and build each other up, just as in fact you are doing.
1 Thessalonians 5:11

One Sabbath, a friend of ours got baptized and I wanted to see him after the service. Somehow I missed him, so I decided to drive over to his place after lunch. He lives north of town, so I started going that way, but when I got to the intersection where I should have turned right, I turned left instead. When I realized what I'd done, I thought I must have been daydreaming or something to have missed my turn. When I got to the next street I was alert and determined not to miss my turn again. I thought, I'll turn there and get going north this time, but the same thing happened. The Lord just shut my memory off and I got going the wrong way again.

I thought, Well, I'll just drive by the place where we used to live and maybe drive by the school. A little way ahead, I saw a man walking with a dog in the ditch and I passed by him. Then I decided to back up and see if it was someone I knew.

I had never met the fellow before, but he didn't want to look up because he'd been crying. He was kind of embarrassed.

I said, "Hello. Do you live here?"

"Yes, we just bought that place back on the road a little way," he told me pointing over his shoulder. We talked a bit and I told him I was just coming from church. He said he'd been in church that day, too.

He said he'd just prayed a while before that saying, "Lord, I've just got to see someone and talk to someone." He said he took his dog out and had only walked about 50 yards when I came along. God worked quite a miracle there. The man's name is John Madgwick and he has become one of my closest friends and prayer partners.

The Hand of God

As I look back on my life, I can see that God has always been leading me. When I was a boy, my family could not afford a radio. My brother Henry had bought a crystal set[2] but he never listened to it, so I used it. It was just a little crystal, about a half inch across. It was in a little tin container. A small length of coiled wire called a Cat's Whisker[3] was used to poke into the crystal set. The crystal set was hooked up to a single ear phone on one end and the other end was hooked up to a bedspring which doubled as an aerial.[4]

I often fell asleep listening to my homemade crystal set. I always seemed to pick up preachers like Dr. Peach, and later, The Quiet Hour with J. L. Tucker. I was blessed by listening to that crystal set all those years. For some time, it was my only means of learning about the world and God's plan for me in it.

As I went through school, the teachers would pick me out and often tell me or show me something inspiring and say to me, "That was for you Ben." In retrospect I know that God's leading was even in those small things. I can't think back to a single time in my life when God wasn't leading me. There were times when I felt alone and times when I felt despair, but I have often felt God's presence in my life. Knowing what I know now, I look back and see that even in the times of my deepest despair, God was leading me all the way.

---

2   A crystal set is the simplest form of AM (amplitude modulation) receiver yet devised. It is an early form of a radio receiver.
3   We used metal guitar strings as replacements if we lost the original wire.
4   Because it was above the ground and connected to the ground by the metal frame of the bed, a bedspring worked well as an antenna.

We invite you to view the complete
selection of titles we publish at:

www.ASPECTBooks.com

Scan with your mobile
device to go directly
to our website.

Please write or email us your praises, reactions,
or thoughts about this or any other book we publish at:

ASPECT Books
www.ASPECTBooks.com

P.O. Box 954
Ringgold, GA 30736

info@ASPECTBooks.com

Aspect Books, titles may be purchased in bulk for
educational, business, fund-raising, or sales promotional use.
For information, please e-mail:

BulkSales@ASPECTBooks.com

Finally, if you are interested in seeing
your own book in print, please contact us at

publishing@ASPECTBooks.com

We would be happy to review your manuscript for free.

www.ingramcontent.com/pod-product-compliance
Lightning Source LLC
Chambersburg PA
CBHW082235170426
43196CB00041B/2798